Common Ground

Common Ground

A NATURALIST'S CAPE COD

Robert Finch

WITH DRAWINGS BY AMANDA CANNELL

W·W·NORTON & COMPANY

NEW YORK · LONDON

First published in 1981 by
David R. Godine, Publisher, Inc.

First published as a Norton paperback 1994

Library of Congress Cataloging in Publication Data

Finch, Robert, 1943 -
    Common ground, a naturalist's Cape Cod.

    1. Natural history — Massachusetts — Cape Cod.
2. Cape Cod. I. Title.
QH105.M4F56   574-9744´92   80-83953

ISBN 0-393-31179-1

Acknowledgments: The essays in this book are reprinted by permission of *The Cape Codder*, *The Provincetown Advocate*, *The Register*, and the *Falmouth Enterprise*, in which they first appeared. They are reprinted here in slightly revised form.

W. W. Norton & Company, Inc., 500 Fifth Avenue, New York, N.Y. 10110
W. W. Norton & Company Ltd, 10 Coptic Street, London WC1A 1PU

Printed in the United States of America

1 2 3 4 5 6 7 8 9 0

*To the staff and members of the
Cape Cod Museum of Natural History,
who helped make these journeys possible.*

Foreword

This is a book about beginnings, or landfalls, in a place by the sea that has been explored, settled, visited, studied, and written about more than almost any other stretch of the North American coastline. Yet despite its long history of intense use, Cape Cod is still essentially, as it was to the Mayflower passengers, an unknown coast. For each individual arriving new on its shores, it offers a place to begin, to stumble, to leave and return to, and finally, perhaps, to stay.

In one sense, perhaps the most important, the specific setting of these essays is incidental. In another, of course, the Cape is a very special place, not only because it is famous as a summer playground, or because of its intimate relationship with the ocean (not all towns have whales wash up in their backyards), but for that peculiar figure it has always formed in the American imagination, a figure at once microcosmic and unique, representative and individual. As a friend of mine once said to me regarding television coverage of our local herring run: 'If it happens on Cape Cod, it's more important.'

For me the Cape has also been a place of unusual accessibility to the natural world and to all that implies, a landscape whose low hills and long shores seem to answer the contours of my own imagination.

The focus of these essays, then, is personal, one man's response to the changing face of this curved peninsula. Their aim is not primarily natural history, nor am I a naturalist except in the sense that nature is the largest object on my horizon, a fact that has gradually led me to learn something about its basic processes. The essays were written over a period of several years with the intent of exploring the idea that, in a global age, it becomes increasingly important to keep in touch, on a direct and personal level, with the place where one lives. I felt that living with nature in the late twentieth century must mean more than turning down the thermostat and meeting state sanitary codes. There is no code for it; nature is not something to co-exist with, but existence itself.

Not only the Cape, but every locale, needs to be measured by the human foot and eye as well as with population graphs and water studies. It needs to be sounded, not merely for its capacity to support human traffic and commerce, but for its seasonal mysteries and secret running life. It needs to be known, not only from soil samples and by planning boards, but in its many moods and expressions, its comings and goings, its various lives and forces that can excite wonder and awe and new ways of seeing. And it needs to be supplied, not just with tourists and oil, but with a love that inspires discipline and commitment from all who use it.

We always undertake more than we know, however, and now these pieces seem to form a record of changes in myself as well, the loose outline of a journey of coming, sometimes flawed, to the natural world. There is also, in the later ones, some attempt to balance human and natural concerns, but only as a beach is in dynamic balance with the ocean that constantly reshapes it.

The road to nature is always a footpath. Whatever environmental ethics one does or does not subscribe to, each individual must come to his or her own terms with the world. Thus most of the explorations in this book were of necessity taken alone.

In another sense, however, no journey is ever taken alone. Besides the help and encouragement received from my family, my friends at the Cape Cod Museum of Natural History, and especially from my editor at Godine, Deanne Smeltzer, this book depends significantly on those who have walked these shores before me: explorers, scientists, historians, artists, the old Cape Codders themselves, and above all, other writers. There are many references to those major voices – unusual in number for a place so small – who have imagined and articulated this landscape in ways that have forever changed the way we look at it: Thoreau, Henry Beston, John Hay, Conrad Aiken, and others.

Yet just as no one can repeat Thoreau's famous walk along the Outer Beach (the route of which is now more than a hundred yards out to sea), so the past, however compelling, is constantly eroding to some degree. The present always calls for fresh eyes, not just to pierce the mystery anew, but because too often what we think we see is not the Cape itself, but merely the surface, and then a false surface: an oversimplified, stereotyped myth of national nostalgia known as 'Old Cape Cod.'

Too much false seeing and false thinking about such a vulnerable land have already caused serious problems, and will cause more if not corrected. They will also take away those rich resources for individual growth that the true natural variety of any place affords. For whatever changes have occurred, however much has been irrevocably lost of the past and those who lived it here, we are always left with what the First Comers had to begin with: the land itself, sea-born and sea-shaped.

Greatly altered in appearance – in places to the point of unrecognizability – Cape Cod nonetheless remains as fundamental, challenging and unexhausted a departure point for discovery and self-discovery as it ever was. After more than three and a half centuries of occupation by Western man, the real Cape still eludes us, offering and withdrawing its mysteries with the tides, saying follow me, know me, live with me.

ROBERT FINCH
Brewster, Massachusetts
February 13, 1981

Contents

Common Ground

Night in a Dune Shack

Others than myself should be writing this. I have been at best an infrequent visitor to the dune country, or what used to be called 'the outback' of the Provincelands. I no longer even live in Provincetown. It would be better done, I suspect, by one of the 'shack people' – those enviable individuals who live among the dunes summer after summer, and even year-round, in those marvelous barnacle-boxes still perched here and there along the outermost line of dunes from Race Point to High Head. Many of them have been writers themselves, ever since Eugene O'Neill worked on his early plays out there in the old Peaked Hills Bar Life Saving Station. It is they who best know that country, those several square miles of sea-spawned, wind-shaped sandhills and valleys, domes and bowls, that sprawl between Route 6 and the Atlantic Ocean at the very tip of Cape Cod – a region once described by Mary Heaton Vorse as 'a little wild animal that crouches under the hand of man but is never tamed.'

And yet I once was touched directly by the dunes in a way that connects me not only to them but to still another writer who lived there. So I want to begin with a personal anecdote, not just as a way of getting into a rather complex subject, but because such stories are important. Behind every passionate interest there is almost always some such story to be found.

Eighteen years ago Provincetown in the winter was a very different place for a young man out of sorts with the world. I had

3

taken a year off from college and worked on the reporting staff of a now-defunct weekly newspaper. In fact I *was* the entire reporting staff, covering the obituaries, whist party winners, Portuguese-American League dinners, high school basketball scores and civil defense meetings that made up the meat of the off-season news in those days.

At that time everyone who graduated from the local high school seemed to be in a hurry to leave or get married. After the summer crowds left, there were few unattached people in the town between eighteen and thirty. It was three months before I got to know another person my own age. On weekends I used to hitch rides up Cape to see friends in Orleans, and between work and these weekly escapes I had had little chance to explore the dunes in back of the town.

One day shortly after Christmas, however, when the paper had shut down for a week, I packed a lunch and walked out of town along Howland Street, across the old railroad bed (railless for years even then, but still paved with ties), across the state highway, up into the oak-covered hills east of Grassy Pond, and finally into the dunes themselves.

I was totally ignorant of their geography then, and went mapless into that country with all the careless assurance of youth, though I was aware of the tall granite tower of the Pilgrim Monument that loomed over my shoulder as a constant landmark, should I need it. I had heard of, and had in part set out to find, Mt. Gilboa and Mt. Ararat, two of the largest of the dunes. I was actually more than a mile west of those sandy summits, but I had no way of knowing that. Nevertheless, the impression of the dune landscape was immediately Biblical, reminiscent of those valleys and desert wildernesses I had always imagined the tribes of Israel wandering through. There is something fundamentally allegorical about the dune country: each feature – every bush, bog, ridge and buried tree trunk – stands out from its background with a kind of concentrated suggestiveness. The scale is small and uncluttered, an expressionist landscape that seems created for parables and myths.

I remember it was a sunny day, for I watched my shadow elongate as I gained each ridge, shoot out across the wide, hollow sand bowls as I chased it down the slopes, then shorten again and slow as I climbed the flank of the next hill. Even then I had a sense of undulation, of the dunes as a series of waves, though I had no notion of their origin or their behavior other than that they seemed very unthreatening and accessible, even on a cold winter's day, to human probing.

Stretched along the outermost ridge were the dune shacks, more numerous than they are now. I spent an hour or more poking around them in idle curiosity, working my way gradually west, where I had some vague idea Race Point Beach lay.

At one point I came upon a shack, smaller than the rest, perched in a little hollow just behind the foredune of the beach. The day had clouded over and was beginning to get chilly. I thought that if the shack were open, I might borrow its hospitality long enough to eat lunch and warm up a bit before heading back to town.

The shack had apparently not been used recently. The door was banked with at least a foot of sand, but was unpadlocked. I scooped the sand away, pulled the door open and entered. This was no ordinary dwelling, even among a community of eccentric structures. Against one wall were two bunk beds, each covered with real bearskin blankets. On another wall a series of rough bookshelves supported an extensive and remarkably eclectic library.

There were esoteric works by Swedenborg and Kierkegaard, a volume of Beethoven sonatas, a large poetry collection (including first editions of Sandburg and Frost), a novel done completely in woodcuts, and cheap nineteenth-century editions of Hawthorne and Dickens. But there were also dozens of paperback science-fiction novels and westerns, many of which I remembered reading in high school.

On the floor were scattered piles of oversized 78 rpm records, mostly classical and operatic selections on old and obscure labels. I picked one up, an original Caruso recording dated 1916, that was completely blank and smooth on the opposite side. The cabin, it seemed, had been abandoned for some time. Sand had seeped in through the cracks in the windows and walls and had formed a thin layer over everything on the floor, including the records. I gathered these up and carefully blew off the sand, wrapped the discs in a towel and placed them on the top bunk.

I stayed beyond lunch, fascinated by this solitary and

quirky outpost of learning, until I realized that it was beginning to grow dark. It struck me that I might spend the night here; there was no reason to be back the next day, I would not be missed by anyone, and no one was likely to come by at night this time of the year. The bearskin blankets looked warm and tempting, and there was a kerosene lamp and even a wood stove that looked in working order.

I decided to stay, and went outside to gather some driftwood to burn. By the time I returned with an armload of wood it was nearly dark. I could still make out the dim looming head of the Monument far to the south, blinking its red aircraft warning lights as though in a final call. But I had resolved to spend the night outside the town. If I should change my mind later in the evening, the tower would always serve as a beacon by which I could steer home any time I chose. I bent my head and entered the dark shack with the wood.

I set about building a fire in the small stove that stood against the west wall. I filled it up with the pieces of driftwood I had gathered, and then noticed that where the stovepipe went through the low roof, the metal collar had rusted out, leaving a gap of an inch or two all around the flue through which sand, wind and rain had poured, badly rusting the top of the stove. I stuffed some rags around the opening and lit the stove. In those days I was innocent not only of natural history but of wood stoves as well.

The wood caught fast enough, but a few minutes later I noticed that the rags I had stuffed around the chimney were beginning to smolder. Quickly I reached for a stick and began to try to dislodge them, but the metal stovepipe, either rusted out or flimsily put together to begin with, came loose from my jabbing and quickly fell apart, collapsing in several sections at my feet.

Within seconds the entire shack was filled with black smoke belching from the top of the chimneyless stove, and I was forced out into the night, stumbling, choking and blind, up onto the dune beside it. I stood there in helpless panic and painful recrimination, certain that at any moment the smoldering rags would ignite the floor, or that the stove itself would burn out, causing the shack to go up in a fiery reprimand to my inept trespassing, a beacon that would bring swift and humiliating retribution out from the town. I had a strong impulse to run as fast as I could back to town, but I was held, as though mesmerized, by what I had started, by the plume of smoke issuing from the hole in the roof, to see what would happen.

Nothing happened. The rags apparently did not catch fire and the kindling burned itself out without mishap. It was fully dark now, and I was cold and hungry in the damp wind, but it was several long minutes before the smoke dispersed enough for me to reenter the shack. When I did, I saw there was no hope of rebuilding the chimney that night. I suddenly felt very tired and drained, more from panic than exertion. I managed to cart the pipe sections and the charred rags outside, stuffed the roof opening with more rags, and set a heavy frying pan on top of the stove hole. Then, resolving that I would leave first thing in the morning before any passing beach buggy or the absent owner should discover me and my folly, I crawled into the lower bunk under the heavy bearskin blanket and sank into sleep like a stone.

When I woke up in the morning, I looked out the window and saw nothing, or nothing I recognized. Thinking it was the smoke that had sooted up the glass, I rubbed it with my sleeve and peered out again. I still saw nothing, but more clearly now, and with a sense of unpleasant surprise. A world of white in motion swirled about the shack. An ocean snowstorm had apparently crept in up the coast during the night (I was innocent of weather reports in those days, too) and had reduced visibility to nearly zero.

I was cold and stiff, and thirsty as well, but I stepped outside into a brisk northeast gale that was racing along the beach toward Race Point. The storm had already laid down some three to four inches of snow which was blowing and drifting furiously about the shack. I could see maybe twenty yards, and there was no sign of the Monument in that dimensionless sky.

With more surprise than anxiety, I found myself somewhat marooned. I had brought no compass, and though I guessed that the storm came from the east, the wind swung about the compass from minute to minute and was probably even more capricious inland. If I were to try heading back to town, I might wander among the featureless dunes for hours. I could have walked west along the beach until I reached the Race Point Coast Guard Station, but I had no idea then how far away it was, a half-mile or five miles. I was trapped more by my ignorance than by the elements.

I decided to make the best of it until the storm stopped, or at least let up. Laboriously, I brought the pipe sections back inside and reassembled the chimney up through the roof. This time I stuffed the opening with a roll of aluminum foil I found in a cabinet, and managed to start the stove again without further trouble.

My supply of wood, however, was not large and not easily replenishable, so I decided the best course was to keep the fire going as slowly as possible and to stay under the blankets to conserve heat. In this manner I managed to spend a not too uncomfortable morning, perusing several volumes of my unknown host's eclectic library and getting up now and then to tend the fire.

By noon, however, hunger began to gnaw at me, and I rummaged through the rough cupboards and drawers near the stove for food. Here I encountered an eccentricity even greater than the library. The only edible items I could find were half a dozen cans of anchovies. I have never liked anchovies, even at parties. Here they seemed like a bad joke, and I put them back, half-disgusted and half-amused, and crawled back into the bunk bed. But in a short while I retrieved one of them, grateful that it had a self-opening key on it. I don't really remember what they tasted like, except that they made me powerfully thirsty, so that I made several trips outside for mouthfuls of snow.

The storm was still going strong at noon, and showed no signs of abating through the afternoon. Several times I considered trying to make it back to town, but decided against it. By dusk, however, I began to get worried. The snow had now piled up to nearly a foot on the beach, and drifted constantly against the east-facing door so that periodically I had to clear it away to keep from being trapped inside. If the blizzard kept up all night, the dunes might well be impassable by morning, or at least very tough going. My wood supply was just about gone, and my clothes were still damp. What if I should come down with chills and fever during the night, and grow delirious?

To keep my strength up I forced down another can of anchovies (and nearly lost it again in doing so), after which I resolved that if, by some cruel fate, I were to die in this crummy place, I would do so on an empty stomach. I dared not waste my flashlight, so I sat there in the bed for several hours in the dark and cold, all charm or interest in the shack long fled, contemptuous and alarmed at the situation I had so innocently fallen into. It seemed now a too-real metaphor of the state of my life at the time, and I wished earnestly only to escape back to what I had been escaping from.

When I finally fell asleep I don't know, but I remember waking joyously in the middle of the night to the unexpected sound of hard rain on the roof. It was my first experience with the capriciousness of the Cape's winter storms, but I seemed to know what it meant, and went back to sleep with a pervading sense of release. In the morning I woke again to see a soggy, ruined, steamy, but suddenly revealed landscape. The snow was almost entirely gone, like a bad dream, and the Monument once again crested the dunes. I followed it back to town like a prodigal son.

Much later, I found out that the shack in which I had spent two nights had belonged to Harry Kemp, Provincetown's famous ex-pugilist and self-styled 'Poet of the Dunes,' who had lived alone there during the last years of his long life. He had died the spring prior to my stay at the age of seventy-seven. Not long after I left, the shack fell into the sea – not, I hope, before someone saved the poet's remarkable library, or at least the Caruso recordings.

Last summer I saw an advertisement for Provincetown's new Heritage Museum that referred to an exhibit of 'Harry Kemp's Dune Shack.' Intrigued, I paid a visit to the museum. The exhibit proved to be a 'replica' of the shack, built from boards and other lumber salvaged when the little house tumbled·into the ocean. It is a curiously compressed, sort of bas-relief affair, built out from the wall less than four feet into the room, and purports to reproduce the interior of the poet's dwelling as it was. But it is not Harry's shack. Everything is too spare and tidy. There are no bunk beds or bearskins, no stove, no records. The only books in sight are a few of Harry's own volumes arranged neatly on a small, plain, wooden desk, as though the only thing writers ever read were their own works.

And there are no anchovies.

Cormorant Ashore

Things are starting to come ashore. This is the time of year for it: mounds of seaweed and eelgrass, ripped from the flats; horseshoe crabs and scallop shells, stranded on the beach; a numbed and bewildered southern sea turtle, two thousand miles from home; the dead but unmarked body of a harbor seal; a sick dolphin.

Now, where human crowds played in the sun a few short months ago, the sea throws up its harvest. Even hard-shelled Thoreau was shaken by the shameless display of death on the Outer Beach and called it 'a vast morgue, where famished dogs may range in packs, and crows come daily to glean the pittance which the tide leaves them.'

A century ago the leavings were more spectacular: hordes of blackfish beaching and wheezing in stinking hundreds on the Bay flats; an occasional stranded whale suffocating itself to death; the up-flung arm of a drowned sailor buried in the sand. Today the sea's offerings may be less appalling, but the message is still clear, if we care to read it.

A northwest wind has been blowing with cool persistence for several days, throwing wide fields of blue and golden light across the Bay, accenting the bright luminescence of the bent and dying marsh grass and the hard brilliance of white-capped water, blue like cobalt. Along the east bank of the creek that flows onto the flats I came upon the exposed ribs of an old wreck that is uncovered from time to time. Its timbers are worm-eaten, held together with large wooden pegs and beaten metal that crumbles into red dust in my fingers. Now the creek flowed out to meet the incoming tide only a few inches deep. These ship bones must have been deposited at a higher and wilder time.

Nearby, on the dryer flats, I saw the remains of a large black bird, a cormorant, one of the larger fish-catchers off our shores. The black webbed feet and the loose gangly wings were still intact, but the upper part of the body had been chewed and eaten away.

I looked down into the bloody body cavity and then followed the long red string of exposed neck vertebrae out to what looked at first like a red hood covering the head. The neck skin had in violence been pulled up over the head, inside out. I peeled it back, revealing the long hooked beak, yellow underneath, and the red throat patch – field marks of the Double-Crested Cormorant. The carcass appeared to have been dragged a hundred feet or so across the sand by a pack of dogs, for there was a trail and a crowd of paw prints around the body.

I pondered the find, not an uncommon migratory tragedy. Double-Crested Cormorants do not frequent the sandy shores of Cape Cod very much, preferring the islands and wharves of Boston Harbor and the rocky coast of Maine for breeding. In summer, however, they may occasionally be seen in the Buzzards Bay area and on the stone breakwaters of Provincetown Harbor (day-trippers from Boston?) in their characteristic pose of hanging their wings out to dry in the sun.

In the fall migratory flocks from the north are sometimes seen flying over the Cape, often mistaken for Canada geese. Most, however, have passed on by the first of November, and I took the mutilated form before me to be that of a straggler, either sick or injured, that had expired en route and been washed ashore by the tide.

But something in the pattern of tracks in the sand was strange. I began tracing the twisting trail back to its source and noticed that immediately the dogs' tracks pulled away from the trail of the bird's body and ran parallel to it several feet away on either side. After about fifty feet the dogs' prints veered off completely, and the body groove continued on its own another fifty feet or so to the spot where it had apparently first come ashore on the previous tide. Here, where the trail started, innumerable bird tracks surrounded it, gulls and others I could not identify, in a silent immobile frenzy.

The pieces snapped together in my mind with a jolt. I did not even have to look more closely at the cormorant's trail to see what I had missed before: the evidence of wing marks beating and feet digging in the wet sand. The bird had been *alive* when it landed, or was left, wounded or sick, by the tide.

The bird tracks said it had been harassed or attacked by gulls and other shore birds. The sands said the bird had dragged itself away in a desperate, twisting flight of a hundred feet or more. In the last half of its attempted escape it had been joined by a pack of dogs that ran beside it, calmly pursuing it across the flats until it either had dropped, exhausted, or was set upon and torn apart into the thing I had found.

The whole story was less than six hours old; in another two it would be erased completely. Suddenly my superficial knowledge of the cormorant's life history seemed irrelevant beside this crushing reminder of the terms of its existence. Here children had played while the summer sun crooned on. Now, a few nearby beach crows looked on disinterestedly at my investigation, waiting for me to leave.

Hurt Junco

Injured birds have a way of humbling us and our pretensions to reparation in the natural world. This is not just because we often lack adequate facilities to treat them. Birds are creatures of extreme delicacy, particularly their bones. They are also finely and complexly attuned to their environment in ways we can only crudely and inadequately approximate indoors. Even if we manage to clean, feed, warm and mend them to the point where their motors seem to be chugging along nicely again, they are apt to give up and die suddenly and inexplicably, throwing us back on our ignorance. Often they seem to die of some requirement we do not even sense, as though to say, I will not be judged or saved on your terms.

One day last fall, before the snows, I found the small inert form of a junco lying on its back on the steps outside our sliding glass doors. At first it looked quite dead. Kneeling down, however, I could see the thin, twiglike legs twitching and the pale pink bill opening and closing slightly. It appeared to be in a state of shock, and I laid the blame on our cat, who occasionally traps a feeding bird and, after toying with it for a while, leaves it for dead.

I slipped my hand under the soft, warm, weightless body and brought it inside the house, placing it in a small box lined with towels near the stove. Within an hour the bird had revived and was leaping about in the box, trying to crash its way out.

I carried it outside again and placed it on the ground, where it immediately tried to take off, but it only succeeded in limping pitifully, though energetically, along the ground, trailing one dark wing and wheeling unbalanced through the leaves until it became entangled in the underbrush. There it stopped, flopped over on its back and lay there twitching and panting as before.

Retrieving it once more, I brought the junco over to our local natural history museum to be examined. I was told that the wing, although not broken, was dislocated and probably would not heal properly. All right. I am as much for natural selection as the next person, but it was I who had marked the fall of this particular junco and I felt somewhat responsible for it. It had been my pet that had injured it at my feeding station. Moreover, however philosophical we try to be, there is something that rebels at the adjuration, 'There is nothing to be done.' Besides, simply to release the bird in this condition would be certain death. So I borrowed a small cage and a book on treating injured birds, brought my patient home, and proceeded to splint up its wing with some pieces of cardboard and cellophane tape.

Few things make you feel more clumsy than attempting to treat a small bird with materials and instruments designed for human proportions. To keep a bird's wing immobile, you must essentially bind up the entire bird. When I was through, the poor junco looked like some ineptly wrapped package, head sticking out one end, feet and tail out the other. Still, the result bore a general resemblance to what the book indicated, and I placed the bird carefully in the cage with some seed and a small jar lid full of water.

The first thing it did was to leap frantically about the cage, scattering seed everywhere, and then flop over on its back, landing in the lid of water and relapsing into that convulsive state in which I had first found it. I scooped it out of the water and placed it on a towel inside the cage, where it recovered in a few minutes. But every time I came near the cage it would have a similar fit and land upside-down in the water again. It seemed to land there deliberately, as though its terror were somehow pacified by having its head in the water, and would stay there until I retrieved it.

At this rate, I thought, it will soon die of pneumonia or exhaustion, so I placed the cage on a high shelf and covered it with a sheet. I heard no more from the bird that afternoon, and in the evening I carefully lifted a corner of the sheet and peered in, not knowing what to expect. The junco was perched on a twig I had inserted and was asleep, a small, gray, fluffed-up ball with its head tucked out of sight, as best it could, into its bound-up wing. It sat there, rocking and heaving rhythmically, like a feathered heart, and I honestly expected to find it dead in the morning.

He didn't die though (it was a male, I later determined), and over the next several days he gradually recovered and soon got accustomed to me so that he didn't go into hysterics every time I approached the cage. But each time I took him out to examine the wing and then replaced him in the cage, he would go into the same act again, ending up on his back in the water dish, from which I would have to retrieve him.

He ate heartily and began filling the house with his sharp little chips, as though complaining that the accommodations weren't any better. During the day I placed him by the picture window where he could watch the other juncos feeding on the ground outside. I wasn't sure whether this was cruel or encouraging, or neither, but he spent a great deal of time watching them intently.

So did I, and I saw some things that made me wonder, first, if I had done our cat an injustice and, second, if I had made too hasty conclusions about the survival capacity of an injured bird. On two occasions, while feeding, the junco flock was suddenly startled by something – not the cat, he was inside – and flew off. Each time, one of the birds flew into the glass doors and seemed momentarily stunned, but recovered and managed to fly away. Perhaps this, and not our cat, accounted for my bird's injury.

About a week after I first found him, another junco which seemed to have an injured wing and could not fly showed up in the flock. This one appeared to be a female (slightly rusty patches on the shoulders, head and breast edges). When I tried to catch her, she hopped adroitly away and hid in an inaccessible part of the woodpile. For several weeks she stayed with the flock at the feeding station, managing to avoid both me and the cat.

She could not fly, and perhaps never would, but for all that she did not exhibit the least sign of Darwinian resignation.

After three weeks of recuperation, I removed the splint and tape from my junco's wing. Immediately he leaped out of my hand and *flew* across the table into the picture window. I knew he wasn't ready to go yet, though, for the wing still drooped some and did not flap as high as the uninjured one. Moreover, in removing the tape I had pulled out a great many of his body feathers and wanted to give him time to replace them.

Back in his cage, but unbound now, he was such a bright, alert and healthy-looking creature that I could not feel sorry for him even in his crippled condition. I found myself thinking that if the wing did not heal properly and he could not fly, he might at least live out his life here with us and for a few autumns greet the junco flock as they returned each October.

Still, I knew he deserved his chance. About a month later, when he seemed to be flapping both wings strongly as he hopped and flitted about his cage, I took him outside once more and let him go. He took off firmly, gained about a foot in altitude, fluttered along erratically for a few yards, then turned over and fell on his back onto the hard ground. He lay there quietly, not in his usual dazed state, but looking at me steadily as I bent down and picked him up.

I brought him inside and placed him right side up in his cage. For the first time in four weeks I found myself talking to him. Not ready to be launched yet, I guess. We'll try again in a few days. And if you don't make it, you're always welcome here. I covered him up with the sheet.

The next morning I didn't hear his usual chips coming from the cage. When I lifted the sheet, I saw that he had not even moved from the spot where I had placed him on the towel, but had simply fallen gently over on his side where he lay now, still as a stone.

The Wilderness Experience

Recently we entertained at our house a good friend who is a dedicated outdoor enthusiast, one who is always urging wilderness upon others and dragging them off to remote corners of New England and southern Canada. When he talks about 'the wilderness experience,' it is as though it were something one could go out and get, like a marriage certificate, if only one were brave and hardy enough.

Unlike marriage, however, there is no official certification that one has indeed experienced wilderness. If anything, it is more like being in love, in that it is just as vague and protean a concept as that other romantic notion, and just as likely to strike unexpectedly and unsought for. Because we have littered the original unbroken wilderness with our artifacts and technology, we think, and increasingly lament, that we have destroyed it. But wilderness is where we find it, or rather, where it finds us. It remains, lurking beneath the veneer of civilization, and unless we are very careful to keep on our designated paths, it is liable to emerge and surround us with sudden and unmistakably wild contact.

One of the greatest losses of bearings I've ever experienced, for instance, was not in some trackless expanse of virgin forest, but in a mere patch of woods, less than two hundred feet across and only a few minutes' walk from Orleans Center. It was several years ago, when I lived alone in a house that stood on a small hill on a side road just off Main Street. Next to the house was a remnant of scrubby woods that stretched down to the street, and whenever I walked into town, I cut through these woods on a single path that ran through them.

So open was the path and so small the woods that, when I used it, I barely thought of going *through* anything at all, let alone a wilderness. With the leaves off the trees, houses and power lines were clearly visible on all sides. The bare, spindly branches were scarcely a visual barrier, much less a physical one.

One evening, I think it was in the early spring of that year, I set off through the woods for the library uptown. Ordinarily I took a flashlight with me when I went out at night, but since there was still plenty of light to see by when I left, and since I only intended to check out a book and return, I didn't bother to take one this time. At the library, however, I fell into a lengthy conversation with the librarian, and it was close to 10 PM when I set off for home.

I walked along under a kind of automatic pilot, my head full of distant thoughts, letting my feet follow the familiar route beneath the street lights. When I reached the woods I unconsciously turned off into them. I was not ten yards along the path, however, when I realized that I wasn't on the path. There was enough light from stars and streetlights so that I could make out the black shapes of trees and buildings, but not enough to show me the way.

As I tried to proceed, the way got more and more impenetrable. I suddenly realized what a tricky little woods it was in a situation like this, because at night, without a light, its obstructions could not be seen. Hidden in the dark, the lower trunks of the pitch pines were spiked with the broken black stumps of dead branches, jabbing at my head. The invisible thorny tangles of bare blackberry vines and leafless catbriar caught at my sleeves and ensnared my legs, and the spindly trunks and twigs of the understory trees lashed out at me without warning.

Had it been summer, and the woods full and leafy, I probably would have been able to make out the open corridor of the path in the dim light. Instead, I felt like a bird in one of those darkened, experimental rooms, strung with wires, that are used to test night vision in owls and bats. I wandered helplessly in an invisible labyrinth of impediments. What by day had been a route so familiar and benign that I had ceased to notice it, was now all at once menacing and totally alien. Though I was certain I was less than a hundred feet from my house, I felt effectively marooned and blind. I suddenly realized that I did not know these woods at all. It was a face I had looked on for months and months, and yet because I had no cause to see it, I found I had not the crudest notion of its features.

Of course, I felt no real apprehension (though I was careful to keep a hand up in front of my eyes). I could, if necessary, have cried out for help and roused my sleepy, bewildered neighbors out of the dark houses that surrounded me. Or, like a bull, I could simply have lowered my head and blindly battered my way out of there, with probably no more consequences than some torn pants and superficial scratches. But I felt too foolish and embarrassed at being so helpless and lost in the midst of so little.

Eventually I stumbled on a large boulder, which I recognized from having examined its lichen one day, so that I had some idea of how lost I was, but not in what direction to go. I sat down on the rock, apparently stymied, caught in a dead-end tangle with no choice but to yell or plow out or sit there till dawn. In utter frustration I looked upward at the night sky – and saw the stars. There was the Big Dipper pointing its dependable pot at the North Star. I realized that I had gotten turned around and was heading directly away from the house. In years of night hiking all across the country, this was the only time I ever used the stars in earnest to tell me direction. Thanks to them, I reoriented myself and with little more trouble was shortly out of that patch of woods whose length I could cross in less than a minute by day, but in whose unsuspected depths I had been wandering in circles for over a quarter of an hour.

Wilderness is where you find it, or perhaps where you lose yourself.

Snowy

She sat and watched me across the barren sandy plain with silent indifferent eyes, as though I were a piece of driftwood. A flock of winter dunlins swept and crisscrossed the marsh behind her, emphasizing her immobility. She was a large bird, more gray than white at a distance, and highly marked –the signs of a female. Her breast was flecked with lateral black markings like those of a great horned owl, and the wing and back feathers were also tipped in black. The head markings started in a widow's peak, then carried back around and down like sideburns over the ear openings. The male, by contrast, is usually smaller and much less marked, often nearly pure white.

This was the first time I had ever seen a snowy owl in the wild and all these details and comparisons did not surface in my mind until much later. At the time I was only aware of watching, and being watched by, one of the most beautiful creatures I had ever seen.

Seeing a snowy on Cape Cod is largely a matter of being in the right place at the right time. These occasional arctic visitors to the Cape's winter beaches are not that uncommon, but their appearances vary greatly from year to year. During so-called 'flight years,' up to fifty or more of these great white birds, largest of all our North American owls, have been reported here.

Ornithologists still debate over the precise causes of these en masse southern migrations, which seem to occur roughly every five years. Still, they appear to be definitely linked with the cyclical abundance of the owls' arctic prey, mainly lemmings and northern hares. An exceptionally snowy winter on their home grounds might also make the rodent food supply less available and thus drive some of the population south. I don't believe that this winter was a flight year, at least not here; but even in off years one or two of these birds can be expected somewhere along our outer shores.

Over Christmas week a snowy had been reported on Nauset Beach a couple of miles north of the Orleans parking lot. One morning after New Year's I drove down to have a look. It was a semi-raw day, overcast, with the wind north-northeast and cold when you headed into it. The ocean had a magnificent, bruised look about it, and pawed at the upper beach with dark, polished claws.

I took the landward route north, walking inside the wall of low dunes up toward the inlet. I saw where a recent northeaster had washed over their crest and spilled considerable beach sand down their backsides, burying the beach grass and then crusting over in the cold, so that the sand continually broke through as I walked over it, as salt ice will on a frozen marsh.

There was not much to be seen on the way out, and I knew that my expectations were based a great deal on faith. With its keen hearing and daytime vision, the owl might easily spot me and slip away long before I saw it. There was also no guarantee it would be on the Orleans spit in the first place. It might have flown across the inlet to Coast Guard Beach, or out to New Island, created a few winters ago when the ocean made a new inlet into Nauset Harbor and sheared off the southern end of the Eastham spit. It might even be gone completely, or have been shot – though it is now a protected species.

I remembered reading that during the great flight year of 1926-27 over 2300 snowy owls were shot and kept as trophies in the United States alone. One of the greatest difficulties for modern conservationists, I think, is to rightly conceive how much we have lost. We trudge so far today to see so little, that the result is often a strangely pathetic elation.

When I came to where the dunes tapered down and ended, the beach spread out into a large, wide, bare plain separating ocean and marsh. Here in summer is a large least tern colony, the area posted and protected from human interference. One owl could wreak unbelievable damage on such a colony, but snowys almost always leave for the north again by March. On this same plain in other winters I have sometimes surprised a flock of a thousand gulls, standing in solemn congregation, and have run among them like a banshee, turning the air into a gray and white screaming turbulence. But today there was nothing, only an empty vastness and a darkening sky.

I stood atop the last dune, where I had an unobstructed view of the sands as far north as the inlet, and looked through my glasses for several minutes. Nothing. My ears began to grow cold and my hopes flagged. I was about to leave and scanned the barren plain one last time. By chance I noticed near a slight rise a light gray post the top of which suddenly cocked over. It was the owl, slouched against a lump of sand with a tuft of grass growing on its top, about two hundred yards off on the inlet side. I walked obliquely but openly northeast across the plain toward the ocean side until I was slightly north of the bird, some hundred yards away, forcing it to look into the wind at me. Then I sat down and looked at the owl carefully through field glasses for the first time.

The owl indolently turned her head from side to side and then deliberately rested her gaze on me. She stared down the barrels of my binoculars with heavily-lidded yellow eyes. The masked face resembled that of a hockey goalie, a ritual mask of hidden strength and violence.

The snowy owl's peculiarly lidded eyes – 'bedroom eyes,' my father calls them – give it a sleepy, dreamy aspect, causing most people who see one for the first time to assume that it is sick or exhausted. It also has a peculiar stance. Unlike most owls, a snowy tends not to perch upright, but leans or slouches over against the ground, almost touching its breast. It will sometimes fish along a stream, lying at full length on its side beside the bank, utterly motionless until a fish swims by and a hidden talon darts out with lightning speed. When at rest everything about the snowy owl suggests sloth and unawareness; it is a beautiful ruse.

On their breeding grounds in the far north these snowy owls are said to possess a formidable and somewhat eerie repertoire of hoots, grunts and barks. But like wise men in strange lands they keep silent during their erratic southern migrations.

In their normal range these birds are not exclusively coastal residents, but it was suddenly clear to me why, when they visit the Cape, they prefer our outer beaches to our woodlands. Here everything conspired to remind her of her northern home. The small sand hummock, in the lee of which she now rested, was a sandy reproduction of the frost-heaved rises, called *pingaluks*, which dot her native tundra. On these pingaluks the owls nest and scan the moss- and lichen-covered terrain for prey. New Island, out in the inlet, was said to have a healthy population of voles, a highly acceptable substitute for arctic lemmings in her diet.

Geese and ducks fed in the water of the marshes beyond her, as they do in the summer-thawed lakes and swamps of the arctic. Earlier that week a friend of mine had watched the owl rip apart the carcass of a Canada goose with her powerful talons and beak on the banks of the island. She had probably found the goose dead, although these four-pound predators have been known to kill, and even fly off with, full-grown geese twice their own weight.

Under her unyielding gaze the plain was transformed into a frozen northern tundra, the sand into windswept snow. The parking lot twenty minutes to the south withdrew a thousand miles away, and I, not the owl, became the intruder and temporary visitor.

Keeping my binoculars trained on her, I began to inch slowly toward her on my seat, hoping that this unconventional or low-profile approach might distract her. If this sounds like a stupid ploy, it probably was; but I had seen it work with other birds. At any rate, the owl let me play my game for only about thirty feet and then lifted into the air on great, white, creamy wings, drifting swiftly and effortlessly south for a hundred yards, where she came to rest on an old beached timber.

This time I crawled toward her on my stomach, hoping to keep below her line of sight. But she soon rose and again sailed south, this time slipping down behind the low dune from which I had first spotted her.

Obviously she was not interested in escaping me, which she could have done easily by flying across the inlet. It seemed I was merely disturbing some comfortable psychological distance within which she would not tolerate me – about two hundred and fifty feet, it seemed. I wondered if this distance might bear some relationship to the effective and hereditary range of an Eskimo arrow.

This time, however, the dune that hid us from each other was high enough so that I might approach her unseen. I headed swiftly toward it, wondering if her keen ears would pick up my footsteps on the hardened sand; but no owl rose. Finally I reached the dune, crawled carefully up its side, peered through the grass on its ridge and saw – nothing. The owl was gone. It was as though the dune were a magician's cloak that had been spread momentarily over a beautiful woman, and then had been withdrawn to reveal her vanished!

I was certain I had been outfoxed – or outowled; that the bird had slipped away between the dunes, skimming low and unseen out over the sands and down the beach as marsh hawks will do. And then I realized that I was watching a remarkable piece of avian camouflage.

Behind the dune and parallel to the beach was a row of upended wooden pallets placed in the sand as windbreaks for many rows of nearly buried but still visible beach grass plantings. On the top of one of these pallets, perched so that her darker, gray-streaked sides lined up with two of the vertical, wind-bleached boards, sat the owl. At first glance she had looked exactly like an extension of the pallet.

Had the ploy been intentional? I was ready to believe it. But I did not have time to ponder the question. As soon as I realized what it was I was looking at and established eye contact with the owl, she once again lifted into the air with no visible effort. This time she passed deliberately and directly over me, heading with slow, deep wingbeats into the wind. As she passed not thirty feet above my head, I had a glimpse of sheer, cool competence sailing by on pure milk-white wings nearly five feet across. The yellow eyes peered down at me as though I might be a mouse or a lemming, and I was very glad I wasn't.

The owl continued north nearly two hundred yards, then stooped and went into a long low sweet glide that gradually slowed to a halt. Stretching out her talons before her, she came to rest in the precise spot by the low hummock where I had first spotted her a half-hour before. Again she turned her head casually and looked at me with faintly contemptuous indifference, as much as to say, 'Well, we can play this game all day, if *you* care to.'

But I had taken up enough of her time. Somehow I had the feeling that I had not seen a snowy owl so much as been seen by one. Certain encounters always turn out that way, whatever the intention. It seems a matter of character. I turned and headed south, back to the car, leaving her to her undisturbed and unchallenged isolation.

Wilderness at the Run

Saturday night a driving southeast storm swept the land, shaking boughs of cherry blossoms to the ground, plastering embryonic oak leaves to our windows and sending up the surf at Nauset. The following morning I woke to a clearing but still unsettled sky, and stopped down at the Stony Brook herring run where I found myself the first visitor of the day.

Our herring, or alewife, run has two fairly distinct, separate waves of migrating fish. The first, referred to locally as the 'bluebacks' or 'blackbacks,' are a variety said to have been imported from the run up at Middleboro over a decade ago. They are darker on top and slightly smaller than the native alewives, and generally come in from the Bay to spawn three to four weeks earlier. After their first surge, the run slacks off somewhat, to be followed in turn by the larger hordes of 'genuine' Brewster herring.

The second or 'real' run has been in for several weeks now, but never have I seen the herring so thick or full of energy as they were that morning. Perhaps the previous night's deluge had something to do with it. I have been told that a heavy rain seems to bring the fish in in greater numbers along some estuaries. Ernest Gage, a long-time member of our local Alewives Committee who has cared for and lived beside this run for many years, maintains that the native fish are naturally more 'aggressive' than the imported brand. Certainly the passion was on them now, a frenzy almost, making the first run seem more like a walk.

They crowded in at the culvert below the road. In the stepped pools of the fish ladder further down, the overflow turmoil of the descending waters was matched by their upward drive. At one rung I tried to count the rate at which they were flowing through. Two or three fish a second, it appeared, vibrated up through the foot-high concrete lock into the next pool. But then I looked up at the next one where they were exploding up the falls in bursts of three, four, five fish simultaneously, a fountain of fish gushing up against the stream.

Taken out of the water, these native alewives have lighter, pinker sides than the 'bluebacks.' But in the falling turbulence their iridescent backs arched and surfaced with glinting, shifting colors intense enough to wreck and founder a watching eye. Occasionally one's driving force upward would exactly match that of the descending current, and for several seconds the fish would remain stationary, vibrating vertically in mid-fall, its glittering image broken apart in the prismatic water like some cubist portrait of a herring.

A few fish occasionally dropped back into the preceding pool. Perhaps they had already spawned and were now beginning their descent back to the ocean. But more, it seemed it was simply from the inability of the pool above to hold the numbers of bodies being thrust up into it. The force with which the fish leaped, or bored upward was often so powerful that it carried them skittering across the surface of the pool above and into the column of the next waterfall. Sometimes they would be slightly deflected and go sliding partway up the dirt bank or a bordering boulder, flopping over and over like living, silvery coins. Or else they might be sprung back and flipped down again into the pool from which they had just come.

Fish were trying every outlet: side streams, impassable falls, even tiny seepages coming out of the old mill race above. The frenzy seemed to be in part a product of their very numbers, a mass excitement communicated electrically among the hordes. I straddled one concrete ladder and watched them explode upward between my legs. There was no break in the progression; my Colossus was ignored. In such a state they are oblivious to everything but flow.

Down below the fish ladder, by a wooden bridge, a side stream which forks off above rejoins the main stream by cascading over a steep rocky precipice. There I watched 'a scene to force the heart,' as John Hay puts it in his book *The Run*. Many of the fish were flinging themselves futilely, blindly, at the impassable barrier. I counted eight dead, twisted bodies strewn on shore and rocks, martyrs to persistence. A few survivors, bewildered and weakened, circled slowly and hesitantly in the water below, as though seeking a way to avoid both death and doubt.

Their numbers that day darkened the waters below the bridge as far as I could see. Each swirl or ripple held its protruding fin. Beyond the first bend rose the din and shapes of the inevitable gulls: hundreds of them perched on the banks, jockeying for position, paddling in the stream like ducks, rising and falling in the air, and screaming like banshees.

I watched them for several minutes, but it seemed they did very little actual preying on the fish coursing through the channel there. They spent most of the time screaming at or pushing each other, or just swimming. Occasionally a bird would thrust its beak into the stream, but I never saw one come up with a fish. Perhaps they were all temporarily sated, either from feeding farther downstream or at the nearby dump. I have seen them at other times attacking in earnest, bearing the draped, transfixed bodies of the silvery fish in their hard yellow beaks. But now they were at most tormentors rather than destroyers. Even more, they seemed to be catching their excitement from the fish themselves, translating the herrings' watery passion into an airborne expression: a visible feathery smoke of that submerged fire.

I walked along the flank of the line of low hills that rise and fall down the west side of the stream valley, herding the gulls in the water noisily before me. When I came to the highest prominence, a bald grassy dome overlooking the valley, there was a sudden rush of wings as a hundred sitting gulls rose up into the air and out over the space below, leaving the down-covered and white-spattered crown to the storm and me.

I looked out over a magnificent, turbulent symphony of wind, rain, circling and interweaving gulls, flowing water and cleaving fins, and a wild mixture of sound that partook of all the earth's shattered and shattering forces. Wildness and wilderness are not, after all, to be evaluated by size or remoteness, but by the nature and play of forces within a place. That morning, at least, the narrow, shallow channel of Stony Brook Valley contained more than its share of creation.

Loon

Loons are one of the regrets I have about living on Cape Cod. It is true that they are common winter visitors off our shores, but these are poor, diminished versions of the breeding birds of northern lakes. By the time the migrating loons arrive in late September off the Outer Beach or cross in small groups over the Canal toward Buzzards Bay, they have already lost not only their splendid breeding plumage, but their voices as well. The birds that come south to us are dull and silent, leaving their essence in the north woods.

Last summer we visited some friends for a few days at their lake camp in western Maine. The camp is an old one, built before World War I and run as a boys' camp by a man who is now ninety-seven and still lives in his house in nearby Frye-burg. The land itself is occupied by tall, straight white pines nearly a hundred feet high and at least that old in years. It is easy to see that the trees have priority here. A recently-built guest house jogs its way around some of the older individuals so that it looks as though the trees are growing up out of its roof. Outside each door and around every corner is a massive, dark pine trunk. The trees clutch the rock beneath the thin soil with their spreading roots, and their scaly bark calmly mouths the edges of outbuildings. One old patriarch has literally en-gulfed six inches of a storage shed's tin roof. I suspect there is not a square foot of their land that does not have a pine root beneath it.

The camp sits on the eastern shore of Kezar Lake, a fine, long, northern lake near the Maine–New Hampshire border. Across its broad waters is a magnificent view of the White Mountains. Maine lakes are not like our Cape ponds. It is not just their size, or the encircling mountains, or the presence of land-locked salmon or the dark border of fir, spruce and pine. The water itself is different. It has a deep, sweet vegetable smell, like a well-watered garden. The waters do not seep slowly into a porous, sandy aquifer but run through rocky channels, constantly flushed and refilled from hills and streams, flowing out into wide, shallow rivers. We arrived at Kezar Lake just after three days of hard rain which had raised the level of the lake half a foot, so that the lily pads, stretched taut on their swaying, stringy stems, floated several inches beneath the surface.

All through the evenings and nights we spent there we could hear the loons calling to one another across the dark lake: wild, wondrous canticles plucked from the lake's bottom on their long, deep dives, balanced a moment in their throats, then flung up toward the stars, the moon-edged clouds, and the dark, brooding shapes of the mountains sliding away, one behind the other, into the steep night. What a noise there must have been when owls sang in the tall virgin pines, when lynx screeched out their passion, and wolves added their howls to the loons' weird wailings!

Occasionally we would hear loons calling during the day as well, far out in the middle of the lake. Loons are the only birds I know of that regularly sing both in daylight and at night, though they are much more active after dark. I sometimes wonder about the nocturnal singers – owls, whippoorwills, loons. What do they know that the others don't? Owls and whippoorwills also feed at night. Can the loon, which is an unsurpassed swimmer and spears fish with its stout, sharp beak, stalk its prey underwater at night?

Loon fossils fifty million years old have been found which are virtually identical to present-day birds. Ostensibly for this reason, and for more obscure anatomical features, loons are considered the most primitive of North American birds, which is why they appear at the front of most bird guides. But taxonomy is largely a human invention, based on a very fragmentary fossil record, and I have often wondered if evolutionary classification isn't influenced, at least to some small degree, by subjective, unscientific factors. The loon's laugh, for instance, has been described by one very respected and sober ornithologist as an 'insane cackle,' and to most people it seems to belong somewhere far below us in the nether regions of time. Is it purely coincidence that there is where the taxonomists have placed it?

Nonetheless, this most 'primitive' bird has a genuine song, not just a toneless sound like the hawk's scream or the blue heron's guttural bark. It has, in fact, a series of songs with a fairly distinct sequence, or so it seemed to me while I was there. Generally the loons began around dusk with their 'trumpeting' calls, long drawn-out sounds not unlike the bugling of a Canada goose, but with a slow, sad dying-off like the opening notes of a mourning dove's song: *OO-AHhoooo*.

These trumpet calls answered one another across the wide dark reaches of the lake until, as though on signal, the loon's famed 'yodeling laugh' would begin, a short, shivering, chuckling leap of a sound that was soon taken up by every loon on the lake.

These are the two loon songs most frequently heard and described, but there is at least one other distinct song which is much more impressive than either of these, though much less frequently given. Perhaps it is the 'storm call' to which some accounts refer, though the ones I heard did not presage any bad weather. This third song begins somewhat like the trumpet call, rising gradually; but instead of ending with the long, descending wail of the first, it breaks out and continues to rise several more octaves in startling, sliding arpeggios, until it reaches an unbelievably high peak and hangs there, barking out a descending two-note laugh over and over – a hoarse, despairing laugh something like that of the herring gull's but much more piercing and poignant.

What this cry means to other loons I have no idea, but when one of the birds launched into it, the others did not take it up but always quieted down, as though it had some special significance and took pre-eminence. The Abnaki Indians of Maine, I have read, believed the loon was their earthly messenger to the Great Spirit. If so, then surely this climactic song represented their plea for the misericorde, a cry for divine release from all worldly travail.

Having listened to these birds for several nights, I decided to get a good look at them by day, to determine that they were not just disembodied voices. The next morning, shortly after six, I canoed along the glassy, mist-covered surface of the lake down to the marshy southern end where they were said to nest. I saw none there, but on the way back I heard, and then saw, what at first I took to be a Canada goose taking off from the western side of the lake. It came straight across the water, wings flapping loudly, head low and threatening, as though it were charging something unseen on the other side of the lake. It thrashed and kicked its way with powerful leg strokes across the surface of the water for two hundred feet or more, and then rose only inches above the water, still on an unswerving course. Only very gradually did it rise and veer slowly, parallel to the lake shore, so that I could see the tapered, spindle-shaped body and trailing legs as it let go its throaty trumpeting in flight.

Finally airborne in earnest after a take-off of nearly a quarter mile, the loon made a long, slow arc around the lower end of the lake, wings chugging like a combustion engine and audible at least a half mile away. When at last it returned to the middle of the lake, it began to descend for one of the inimitable loon landings. At first it looked like a goose or duck coming in, braking itself with arched wings, ready to thrust its legs forward like landing gear. But at the last moment it threw its whole body forward and belly-flopped onto the water like a penguin sliding across ice, stabilizing itself with its large keel bone until, after skidding well over a hundred feet, it finally came to a stop.

The loon is a heavy bird, up to fifteen pounds, and though its wingspread is nearly five feet, the wing area is small in proportion to its weight. Loons are designed more for the denser medium of water and need wide margins for maneuvering in air or for making transitions between the two. It is not only a love of solitude that makes them seek these large northern lakes.

Soon after the first loon landed, a second joined it, its mate presumably, passing less than fifty feet above my canoe and splashing down in the same way. Even when gliding in for a landing, the loon's motionless wings produce a very loud, rushing sound. The second bird ended up about a hundred feet from the first, and immediately they swam directly toward one another and circled about, beaks pointed together and tilted upwards, almost touching. The stylized, geometric, black-and-white patterning of their breeding plumage heightened the sense of ceremony in this simple greeting behavior. After a minute they dove together and, with no apparent concern for me, gradually worked their way out of sight behind a small, wooded island where I guessed they had their nest.

Loons breed on both coasts and all across Canada. During the days of unregulated hunting they were heavily shot during migration. They survived on their isolated breeding grounds, however, and since the early part of this century they have been making what is termed a 'precarious recovery.' But lately there have been disturbing signs of a reversal, and loon numbers in the Northeast have been plummeting. The inevitable sprawl of lakeside developments, marinas and motorboats, hydroelectric plants, and an increase in predators such as raccoons and skunks associated with human dwellings appear to be chasing the loons from many of their ancestral northern homes. Never a common breeder in Massachusetts, only one nesting pair was reported this summer. Even more alarming is an Audubon census which shows that in the entire state of New Hampshire, a traditional breeding area for loons, only thirty-six loon chicks were success-fully raised during the summer of 1978. The loon, it appears, not only prefers its solitude but, less compromising than we are, demands it as a condition of its existence.

There are a few reports that loons did once nest on the Cape, well over a century ago. I would like to believe it and could wish again to see their powerful flight and to hear their hollow, mirthless laughter over our local ponds. But having listened to them in their northern setting, it seems unlikely, or at least inappropriate. A loon could no more sing on a Cape Cod pond than a box turtle could hiss on the arctic tundra. They draw their notes from those long, deep, mountain-channeled waters and throw them against the surrounding slopes and the tall trees. It is a song that calls for an echo, and gets it. It is there they most belong, on those dark northern lakes, lifting their high turning cries on summer nights over the fragrant pines and the solemn hills.

Roofing

For some reason, autumn always spurs the climbing instinct in me. More than once, at this time of year, I have startled friends and companions by suddenly taking off, squirrellike, up a tree, an abandoned radio tower, or onto a roof. Perhaps it is just a seasonal reaction against having been immersed in the heat and lassitude of summer, a feeling of stagnation, and a desire to get new perspectives, fresh air. Mountains being in short supply on the Cape, I am forced to resort to whatever modest altitudes I can find here.

The best perspective for this season, I am convinced, is a roof. I will use any pretense to get up on one, even money. For several years I had something of a sinecure in this respect, for I worked as a carpenter with a man who had an uncanny knack for finding us roofing work in the fall, and moreover, roofing work with a water view.

On a roof in October on Cape Cod overlooking water – I can't think of a better place to be. There the wind scours the dust and debris of summer out of the eyes and ears, and scrapes the skin clean, so that you feel your senses have been reborn. There the air is sharp and bracing, the light richly altered, and the colors of the land and water searingly pure.

We have lost something, I think, with the regrowth of forests over most of the Cape during the last century. For this view I crave must have been commonplace to most natives here, when the entire Cape was a roof, when its treeless hills and rolling moors provided an unimpeded and horizon-circumscribed view whenever a farmer stopped for a minute and lifted his eyes from his scythe or cranberry scoop.

One fall in particular, I remember, we worked on a rooftop on a high bluff overlooking Nauset Marsh. It is an area crowded with summer houses, but by late September most of the residents are gone and there is little activity left in the neighborhood save that of the roofers. (Carpenters commonly get the best of most dwellings anyhow, experiencing them from the ground up and leaving only the enclosed husks for the owners to occupy merely.) We are, in fact, a kind of seasonal rooftop species, like the mockingbirds that abound there, flitting out of the flame-shaped cedars and skirmishing about us for possession of a treetop, a telephone pole, or a row of uncut, ridge shingles. There they would perch as we worked, singing and shitting at the same time, as though all expressions were equally pleasurable to them.

It is a noisy business for the most part, roofing – ripping off the old shingles, pounding on the new, with a loose rhythm of hammers echoing from roof to roof. It is also said in the trade that carpenters get to talk to plumbers, electricians, masons and others in the building profession, but rarely to each other. Generally this is true, but fall roofing provides something of an exception. Frequently there were two or three crews in the area and, by unspoken mutual agreement, when one crew stopped for coffee or a smoke, so did the others.

Then, since we were within easy shouting distance of each other, a brief vocal community would materialize and exchanges would bounce back and forth from rooftop to rooftop, the kind of casual, relaxed banter that springs up between bullrakers spread out in the Bay, or that must have occurred between the old-time dorymen bobbing out there alone in their fragile pods on the vastnesses of the Grand Banks. In comparison, our positions were not very risky and our catch was fairly secure, but there was that same shared sense of space and freedom and separateness in a magnificent setting.

Often, when I walked across the ridge, scanning our superb view of the salt inlet, the outer beach and the ocean stretching beyond, I felt like dancing. I wanted to use my hammer to hail the other crews across the empty yards and cedars and rooftops, exclaiming in some antique noble tongue – *Ho! Are we not fine! Where is our like today! Who cannot fail but envy us!* – but, of course, I never did. Most of them, I suspect, also felt this elation at times but kept their seemly counsels. Others, I'm afraid, might just as well have been grubbing in the cellars, stopping up sewage leaks, for all they seemed to take note of the day and their luck. One did hail me once, spontaneously – but what he wanted was the ball scores.

From a rooftop all sorts of incarnate grace appear. Once I saw a remarkable spectacle out over the waters of the marsh. It was a sparkling day, with a few beach-buggy fishermen out on the points of the inlet, and the gulls spread out, white and black, on the marsh islands, perfect in the blue waters.

During a break from the cutting and ripping, I noticed a small flock of late-gathering terns, thirty or forty, appearing over the beach and moving out, westerly, over the waters of the inlet. They flew in a loose circular mass, and regularly those in front would drop down, strike the water for a fish, and rise up again to take their positions at the back of the flock.

They had evidently found a school of small fish and were following it as it moved slowly across the cove below us. As they moved toward me, more and more terns gradually joined the flock, so that it grew, like a snowball, into a mass of more than a hundred birds. It seemed to function carefully, like an organism or a machine, the front rank of terns dropping down and diving beneath the water, then rising up to the rear, followed in turn by the next rank, and the next, and so on. It gave a curious circular motion to the entire flock. They were *reaping* the inlet, like some vast watery combine, but with a complex of psychic and visual relationships of which our machines seem only crude imitations.

From the roof the weather itself seemed more varied and broader in scope – as it does from the prow or mast of a ship. There were many fine days, clear and smooth, that would sail through the golden arc of the sun like a milkweed seed borne on the wind. Others would be rainless, yet wild, tumultuous and brooding, so that the roof seemed to list. Clouds hung low and dark on the east, with a strange reddish light on the horizon, a cold impending light as though the ocean were about to ignite. And there were days when whole ages of weather would pass in a morning, epochs and cycles of light and cloud racing and scudding and mixing overhead as I nailed one shingle. Eternity would pass over, and my hammer would hang in mid-air, suspended. Like Thoreau's bluebird, we carried the sky on our backs and time itself became transfixed, immobile, in the shadow of such glory.

Or so it seemed. Sometimes I think our business is to put ourselves in such favorable positions, open to the sky, where, doing some useful and unimportant work, the poetry of life can catch us unawares. Down off the roof, back on the ground, we are usually too timid and embarrassed of our own possibilities to admit such potential transcendence. We will not admit it to each other either, and so we go on banging temporal stability together – in the form of porch roofs, paychecks and automobile payments – in the face of such manifest presences. Only from such stations of unimpeded view, it seems, are we willing to make those unthinkable, unanticipated leaps into the unknown (or is it the too familiar?) which includes us, to go inside, to the inner fire, and watch creation burn.

The Uses of Wind

One wet, brooding, windy afternoon last week I took a walk north from the Doane Rock picnic area in Eastham along an old wood road that soon petered out among thick stands of pitch pines. I must have wandered for close to a mile without seeing a person or a house, save for one chimney glimpsed over the treetops.

This area was part of the writer-naturalist Henry Beston's 'belt of wild, rolling, and treeless sand moorland' that ran inland from the beach for nearly a mile only fifty years ago. Even then, however, the pitch pines had established themselves well enough further inland so that, as Beston observed, 'people on the outer Cape have their woodlots as well as inlanders.'

At one place I came out of the woods into an old meadow, generously sprinkled with well-spaced junipers, or red-cedars, and broad, lacy, wheat-like stands of young locusts. Though the field was ringed heavily with pines, it is these two other pioneer species that seem to seed in first in this area of the Cape. The locusts had nearly completely lost their leaves, but the dark green junipers were lit up with bunches of bright electric-blue 'berries.'

These shot-sized fruits, an oddity among evergreens, are really modified cones, since the seeds remain technically naked, rather than enclosed in ovaries as in deciduous berries. Yet Rutherford Platt, a man magnificently obsessed with trees, sees in these juniper berries an evolutionary trend, an example of a conifer gradually altering its nature to adapt to conditions of the hardwood forest, perhaps producing in time 'a forest more stalwart than the coniferous, more lovely than the deciduous.'

It is very difficult to feel the reality of such evolutionary drama, impossible to slow or speed one's eyes up enough to catch a sense of motion. We can only apprehend it mentally, imaginatively, and I do not know enough to say for certain what the cedar might be up to, back here in this neglected field. I reached out and crushed its berries, smelling the sweet, incense-like aroma. Were I more of a drinker, I might have recognized in it a common flavoring for gin. What marvelous opportunists we are! Here is this tree, on a slow and stately march toward some unimaginable future, and we pinch its fruits to spice up our booze.

At one end of the meadow was a stand of dead pines, with no oaks grown up beneath them. Their dead, truncated forms swung stiffly in the wind, like gallows. There was no sign of fire, and they were not low enough to have been flooded out. Nearby stands seemed healthy. What then? A local infestation? Had the trees simply overtopped their protection and been withered by the winter salt winds? Nature, like human history, does not tend to record its failures.

Most of the field was marked out with flags of milkweed pods, the open ones all but scoured out now by the wind. Others still remained closed and green, warty and grotesquely bulbous in shape. Milkweeds seem to be among the last of the tall, stiff field weeds to fall; the banners of the mullein and sumacs have been down for weeks. Most of these were the common milkweed (*Asclepias syriaca*) but there was another species present, the wavy- or blunt-leaved milkweed (*Asclepias amplexicaulis*). This plant also likes our dry, open fields, but is somewhat smaller, with rounded, wavy-edged leaves and smoother, more slender, reddish-brown pods.

I lay down in the field beside the plants to study them more closely and to feel, under the open sky, the uses of this dry wind. I watched the gusts tease the seed silks out of the split pods and send them shooting like bits of fleece into the air, where they vanished almost immediately. When I was a boy we used to call the detached silks 'money makers' and would chase them across gritty vacant lots and graveled playgrounds more as a physical challenge than an earnest pursuit of quick fortune. I think we sensed in that buoyant, passive energy, that ground-less good spirits with which the seedless silks went bouncing along, our own childhood faith in wishes that is so completely independent of any need for fulfillment.

The milkweed seeds themselves are brown, thin and light, like pine seeds, and are packed inside the pods in overlapping rows like shingles, with careful, geometric economy. I later took one of the slim pods home with me and placed it on my desk with other accumulating odds and ends from my walks. I forgot about it, but about four nights later I turned on my desk lamp and found that the pods had split open. The seeds had risen up on their own like souls at judgment in their silken garments, had spread them into wings, and had spilled and flowed out over the desk top, waiting for wind. I picked one up and dropped it from head height; in the perfectly still room it took over twenty seconds to reach the floor.

But back there in the field, under the racing, backlighted clouds, where the pines shook, the oaks rattled, the cedars bent over like topknots, and the locusts boomed and shuttled the wind, the broken milkweed pods sent off their bursts of life into a breeding sky. That afternoon the meadow belonged to the plants. The field was vegetably alive, trembling with dispersal and exposure, while all animal life, for all I could see, remained hidden, huddled and perched against the season's blasts.

Foxes on the Marsh

There are signs that the Cape's red fox population is increasing. After suffering from an epidemic of mange disease in recent years, the foxes appear to be recovering and, in some places, proliferating. Two springs ago a litter was successfully raised directly beneath a wooden footbridge that crosses a tidal creek in the Pochet Marsh area of East Orleans. Since then there have been numerous fox sightings all along that part of Nauset Beach.

Earlier this spring I had the opportunity to work for a few weeks on a house being built near the marsh on land that was formerly part of the old Mayo duck farm. It is a lovely site in a small hollow flanked by two conical kame hills, that looks out on the wide lush meadow of the marsh, pocketed with old sloughs and veined with small creeks. Peninsulas of shrub and cedar forests poke out into the marsh on the far side. A heavily wooded slope lies to the north, and eastward the southern tip of the Nauset Beach parking lot can be seen. Southward stretches the long line of the North Beach barrier dunes, their sculptured backslopes rippling with shiny new beach grass like the coat of some healthy animal.

As we worked framing the house in the early weeks of May, small groups of yellowlegs would sweep in with loud descending whistles and probe in the soft mud of the sloughs. Marsh hawks and kestrels soared and hovered over the salt hay,

41

scouring it for marsh rodents. In the late afternoon, when the tide came up from Pleasant Bay and filled the creeks, terns would appear and feed on schools of minnows that rippled beneath the surface like wind-scatters. Occasionally a few Canada geese grazed in the marsh grass near old cedar posts that still stand, marking the limits of the old duck farm fence.

One morning, as we were raising the walls, we spotted a fox making its way up from the south across the marsh. It was a handsome beast about the size of a poodle, but its long, thick, white-tipped tail seemed to lend stature to the rest of its small body. Red foxes show a wide variation in color. This one was reddish in front, shading to a dark gray on the back, flanks and rear legs. It cantered along at an easy lope across the salt hay, heading toward the clump of woods on the northeast edge of the marsh. In its mouth it carried something about the size of a rabbit.

We all lined up between the studs to watch. It seemed to hear rather than see us, pricking up its ears and turning toward us. Instead of crouching or bolting, however, it took only casual notice of us and then proceeded on without haste. In fact, after going a few more yards, it set down its catch and began to rummage around in the marsh, having perhaps sensed a shrew or other marsh rodent. In that manner of hunting characteristic of foxes, it would suddenly pounce, leaping high in the air and coming down with all four paws in the same spot.

After several minutes the animal picked up its catch again, leaped effortlessly across a four-foot ditch and headed toward the hillside. At the edge of the marsh it was met by a young pup about half its size, lighter in color than its parent and reddish all over. The fox gave it a piece of the catch, and the pup trotted off with it back into the woods while the adult stayed out on the marsh and lay down to work on its portion without so much as another glance in our direction. Not a nail had been struck for fifteen minutes. We took no coffee break that morning.

The next day I went out early before work to see if I could discover further signs of the foxes. I walked along an old overgrown road that skirted the north edge of the marsh and made my way up into the briary, overgrown hillside at the point from which the pup had emerged. There I found eight den holes within a hundred fifty feet of each other. Most were freshly dug and one had a definite animal odor at its mouth. One fox family will often dig several dens in a breeding season, moving the young pups to a new one if the vixen feels they have been discovered.

The den entrances were surprisingly small, about a foot wide and eight inches high at the mouth, but tapering down to less than ten inches by five inches before they bent out of sight. The mouths of fox dens are kept scrupulously clean. There were no visible signs as to which, if any, were presently occupied. They were placed fifteen to twenty feet up the slope, so that they commanded a view of the marsh to the south and yet were hedged in with thick undergrowth and brambles. In another week the leaves would be out and the dens completely invisible.

I continued east to the far side of the marsh, skirting the edge of the empty town parking lot, then walking out onto one of the fingers of shrub and cedar forests that protrude into the marsh from the backside of the dunes. These miniature forests appear to have developed on old overwash fans, layers of sand carried through breaks in the dunes during some severe storm in the past and deposited on the marsh behind them. When the dunes heal themselves and build up again, these fans are protected and may eventually develop sizable communities of salt-tolerant shrubs and trees. In time, as the dunes of the barrier beach retreat, these forests will be buried in sand and will form the basis for a new line of dunes.

Such marsh peninsulas are alive with small mammals. I found evidence that this one was a favorite hunting spot for the foxes. There were several piles of rabbit fur strewn about, a seagull wing and several small rodent bones. In addition there were thick stands of beach plums with which the foxes, being in large part vegetarians, would supplement their diet later in the summer.

Coming back past the hillside of dens, I happened to glance up and see the pup sitting at the entrance of one looking straight at me. Its tail was wrapped around its front like a cloak and its fur appeared very light, nearly blond at the edges. Though less than fifty feet away and small as a terrier puppy, it showed no fear and stared at me with adult composure and impersonal curiosity. Only when I lifted my field glasses to my eyes for a closer look did it rise up slowly and without haste saunter back up over the ridge out of sight. On the tree next to the den where it had been sitting was tacked a small sign which said, 'No Hunting.'

The third morning, when I arrived at work at the house, there was a ground fog over Pochet Marsh, what some of the older natives used to call Jack-in-the-mist. By 9 AM it began to break up, sliding and drifting apart like floes of ghost-ice, and revealed a marvelous sight. Once again the hammers stopped and we stood watching from the rafters.

Spread out on the new green of the marsh hay was an entire fox family, two adults and four pups, in full view. The vixen and her pups were together on one side of the little tidal creek, near the edge of the marsh, while the father sat alone on the other side, watching them. The female was colored like the male, reddish in front, shading to dark gray, nearly black, on her rear parts, with a long, thick, white-tipped tail. The pups were all reddish-blond, like the one I had seen the morning before sitting by its den. The mother lay on her side licking one of the pups all over, while a second stood nearby waiting its turn. A few yards away, closer to us, the other pair were play-fighting and rough-tumbling in the wet, glistening grass.

Once again there seemed no doubt that they were all aware of us. We could bang on the plywood and get their attention for a few seconds, but they seemed to have almost no interest in our presence. At one point the male wandered over on his own and looked up at us, less than a hammer's throw away, but he stayed less than a minute and trotted back to watch his family some more. It was as though we were watching dolphins at play from a ship's rigging on a sea of green. The marsh was safe, foreign to human traffic.

After a bit the two pups closest to us stopped rough-housing and walked over to the edge of the creek, directly across from their father. He made no move or gesture toward them and they stood for a while on the muddy bank, poking tentatively at the water with their small paws. Then the more adventurous of the two leaned back and leaped out over the creek, disappearing with a loud plop and emerging a few seconds later on the other side, half its former size and looking like a weasel, soaked and dripping but parading proudly around its father as if to say, 'Well, here I am, Pop.'

Its companion, apparently seeing no reason to get wet just to be second, wandered off to explore the hillside behind it. Meanwhile the first pup left its father and trotted up toward the parking lot to investigate the garbage bins, and was soon joined by a third. The last pup, after receiving its licks from its mother, also disappeared into the woods.

The vixen followed after them a few steps and then, apparently satisfied, turned and flowed across the creek to join her mate. It now appeared to be the parents' hour. Children gone, the two adults lolled on the grass together, licking, scratching and playing with one another in the sun. It was beautiful watching these animals at play in their chosen arena. And what a fine place they had chosen! The dens were on a heavily wooded, well-drained slope with a southern exposure and a commanding view of the marsh. There were plenty of berry bushes and old fruit trees about to feed on. The marsh was filled with rodents. Rabbits and birds abounded in the cedar forest islands to the south. Being primarily nocturnal predators, they would feast all summer as well on the trash and debris in the adjacent beach parking lot.

Even with such abundance, though, I wondered if they sometimes told each other stories, old fragments and legends, hints and sniffs from their ancestors, of a golden age of foxes that once existed here, of a time fox-generations ago when these hillsides, now sites for expensive view-hungry houses, once swarmed with thirty thousand ducks and chickens – fat, flightless, feathered meals protected only by flimsy fences, the posts of which still stick up, like ancient monuments, out of the marsh mud.

After a while the fox pair rose up and, without a glance toward us or the den site, trotted off side by side across the marsh toward one of the cedar islands to the south where they would hunt or rest till evening.

We felt greatly fortunate, of course, to have witnessed such a scene, one of those perfect natural moments that I think subtly changes the relations between those who watch them together. And yet, even as I watched with delight, I knew there was another side to it. Just as the local chicken and duck farmers once worried about foxes, so the apparent recovery of these animals in this area is a matter of some concern to those interested in local birds.

These same foxes pose a threat to the large least tern colony located about a mile and a half to the north on Nauset spit. The terns, a threatened species on the Cape, suffered heavy egg and chick predation from fox last summer, and the situation could be even worse this season. The threat, of course, is not the foxes' fault, for terns have gotten along well with their predators here for hundreds, probably thousands of years. Man's disturbance and development of the terns' breeding areas, however, have forced them into a few abnormally concentrated and vulnerable colonies, so that natural fox predation has, in some areas, become a critical factor that may tip the balance toward extirpation of the terns. Terns, in a sense, have become managed birds and, like the ducks, must now be protected from certain natural predators if they are to survive.

Thinking of these things, I wondered if we have so far mishandled our land that we must now make some final choice between terns and foxes? If we save one, must we eliminate the chance of seeing what I had just witnessed? They owned this marsh and this morning, these animals. They had given me a piece of it and then, like the dawn, had dispersed into day. How do we go about putting a value on such encounters? How many terns is it worth to see a fox family at play in the sun? Is the measurable always to take precedence over the immeasurable?

Countless other lives use this land, its woods, fields, beaches, marshes, creeks, ponds, inlets and dunes – lives unseen and unrecognized, for the most part, under the veneer of our so-called domination of the landscape. I do not know what wilderness is, but I know that it still exists here, often without our approval and in spite of everything we have done to eradicate it. And I know that one of its essential qualities is surprise, the free play of its components. A managed game preserve may produce the largest and healthiest flocks and herds, but if it is managed to the point where it lacks surprise, then it is nothing more than a spacious zoo or a duck farm. I go to a zoo to observe animals, but I go to wilderness to enter a world not mine, where my standards do not apply, where imagination runs in the fur and the flesh and calls to me in a language I cannot decipher but which is nonetheless nourishing and irresistible.

Tide Fingers

While walking along the inner edge of a salt marsh the other day, I stopped to watch a finger of the incoming tide poking its way up one of the dry creek beds. It seemed like something alive, inching and probing forward, twisting and sliding among the interlaced ripple channels, veering off to one side and then the other, halting momentarily as though coiling and gathering strength, then striking out in a long, slow, sinuous glide for several feet.

Looking more closely, I saw that the lengthening, watery digit was populated. A hermit crab was scuttling about near its tip, a small marsh shrimp clambered over the sand grains just behind the crab, and behind the shrimp some sort of long, thin marine worm weaved its way along – all encased, like the organelles in an amoebic cell, in this moving, transparent finger of water.

The tide, advancing across the flats and up creek channels, often does this, creating numerous temporary marine aquariums, spreading out, for our approval and investigation, more organisms than we could assemble with a good deal of time and effort. Similarly, when it recedes, it often leaves its collections of shells, plants and dead animals in the channels between the ripple marks, laid out neatly in parallel rows as though on museum shelves.

I played with the hermit crab a little, prodding him with my own finger to the very limit of the advancing tidal probe. He appeared frustrated that he could not run ahead any faster than his medium of escape was progressing, and tried to retreat, only to be blocked by a dark swatch of seaweed. I tossed him a few inches ahead of the moving channel and he stood there, rocking indecisively, as though he did not know his way back to the water and had to wait for it to catch up with him.

As I stood watching these creatures trapped within the thin, probing edge of the tide, the finger itself ceased to advance and stood there, marking tide, as it were. This was high tide, marked and underscored with a precision and definiteness impossible on the rhythmic, oscillating shores of the outer beach. It was as though the water itself pointed and said, 'Here I stop – no further.'

After no more than a minute, it began visibly to withdraw, leaving a narrow, winding, moist trail in its wake. I had that sense, as Emily Dickinson once did in the presence of the withdrawing tide, that we live, or survive, at the indulgence of some great global courtesy, a net of seemliness or manners thrown over the earth's blind and wrathful forces, a primitive lust of the sea for the land checked by some overriding decorum that we call the regularity of the tides.

And then I saw, for the first time graphically, that strange property of the tide born of planetary inertia. Even as the long finger of the tide withdrew back down the creek bed, innumerable bits of seaweed and other marsh debris continued to be carried *forward* inside it, like a separate flow of arterial blood. The tide has two separate components, one vertical – which we call the rise and fall – and the other, less obvious and horizontal – which is known as the ebb and flood, or current, of the tides.

The first of these two motions is caused by the bulge of the ocean's waters outward toward the moon (and to a lesser extent, the sun). The second motion is the apparent backward and forward movement of the water as the earth's ocean floors turn beneath it. The extremes of the rise and fall motions are called high water and low water, while the turning point between flooding and ebbing currents is known as slack water.

In the open sea, these two movements are indistinguishable. But in harbors, estuaries and flats there may be up to an hour's difference, or lag, between high or low water and slack water. Thus, on our shores, the tide actually begins to fall while it is still flooding, and to rise while it is still ebbing. Yet only in certain protected places, such as the upper reaches of tidal creeks, can the interaction of these two great natural forces be observed so distinctly, unconfused by the competing spectacles of waves and crashing surf.

If this double movement of the tides sounds complicated to us, it can deceive its inhabitants as well. Treacherously, silently, appearing to continue inland even as it withdrew, the finger of tide had moved out, stranding the creatures it had carried in with it. The hermit crab stood with a puzzled air, the shrimp began some ineffectual burrowing, and the worm writhed out its life on the wet sands.

Anthropocentrically, I chose to save the crab (it has 'arms') and tossed it several yards downstream. But when I looked again at the 'worm,' I saw that it was actually a pipefish, a relative of the seahorse and a common inhabitant of eelgrass beds where its eellike body is invisible among the waving grass stands. I picked it up and tossed it along with the crab, and then, just to be catholic, threw the prawn after as well.

I am fascinated by all of the various ways the tides approach our shores: the small, relatively inconsequential fluctuations of Vineyard Sound, the strong, treacherous rips and channels around Monomoy and Woods Hole, the greater height and heaving advance of the Outer Beach, and the impressive sweeps and withdrawals across the wide flats of Cape Cod Bay. Yet whenever I think of the tide it is always like this, as a slow-moving finger of shallow water across grooved sands. I think it must have something to do with the first time I saw the tide come in – I mean the first time I *saw* it, and sensed in its inanimate force that our shores were something alive.

It was in Provincetown Harbor, one summer night many years ago. I was walking the dark shore with a friend, a large, affectionate man with a child's passion for showing people things. We walked in half-lit shadows, behind the Crown and Anchor Inn, in the sallow naked glow of the building's backlights, with the muted noise of whatever dance music was in fashion that season blaring in the background. All at once my friend stopped, pointing down at our feet, and said, 'There it is.'

I stopped, too, looked down, and jumped back in alarm, as though a basket of snakes had been spilled out at my feet. It did look like snakes – small, sliding serpents of black water, twisting and thrusting and sidling across the dark sands, intertwining, separating, and finally coalescing to the rear as it ate up that beach under the piers in small, advancing nibbles. I could not have been more startled and amazed than if I had witnessed the famous tides of Southern France that come in over the flats with the speed of a race horse, or the incredible Amazon tidal bore, a moving waterfall twenty-five feet high and several miles long that moves up the river at twelve knots for some three hundred miles, with a roar that can be heard inland for fifteen miles.

There are times in our lives, decreasingly so as we get older, when we seem peculiarly open to certain impressions. No one can predict these times, nor can we always successfully analyze them afterwards, nor does the force of the impression necessarily bear any proportionate relation to the object that made it. Just why the tide impressed me so that night I do not know. But it has stayed with me ever since, so that when I think of the tide – as I might think of God or Communist China or some other large abstraction – it is not as some great lunar heave and splash of the planetary bathtub, or as some massive, rising inundation, or as any other of its more majestic and dramatic incarnations; but as an intimate running and feeling of water snakes and water fingers across dark sands, an intricate consumption of the land by water, a loving and almost passive tracing of the earth's contours by the advancing sea, taking on those contours, flowing into her curves and edges, even as it obliterates them.

Somehow, in this gentle movement of the tide across the ripples and channels of the flats, I sense the advance of whole oceanic waters across the continental shelf, roaring silently through submerged canyons, across drowned plains and river valleys, taking bends and turns along our crenulated shorelines, funneling up into bays and estuaries, spilling through channels and sinking into holes – so that it meets itself hours apart on either side of Monomoy's thin spar, and with heads so different at each end of the Canal that it creates currents in excess of eight knots every six hours in alternating directions.

Over the years I have watched these delicate fingers of tide push their way along, slowly and thickly, in and out, like summer and winter. So fragile do they seem that I can change their course or block their passage momentarily with my own fingers, as we easily melt the first snowflakes of winter on our palms.

Yet they have behind them the power and inevitability of suns and satellites in their orbits, the force of the world's oceans and the mass of the moon. The actual drops of water in their deft, searching tips may have come in no more than a few hundred feet offshore, yet they have the knowledge of all drowned earth in them. This soft tidal probe is infused with the running of thousands of miles across unknown complexities of terrains, the visible resultant of an untraceable intercourse between sea-bed and sea-heave. It is the moving finger of universal forces that writes, here on these shallow summer sands – inspired, passionate holy water.

Woodcock Flight

his happened last spring, after a day spent walking the power line right-of-way along the string of morainal hills from Barnstable to Orleans. I had set off that morning at Cumma-quid, crossed Yarmouth and Dennis, and did not enter Brewster until late afternoon. I hiked the kettle holes of West Brewster, the high ridges along Setucket, forded the still-icy waters of the narrows where the power lines sweep out grandly over the Mill Ponds, skirted the wasteland of the trailer park along the north shore of Griffiths Pond, climbed the cedar dells of an old farm off Tubman Road and detoured around the fences of the Bassett Wild Animal Farm as a herd of pale, statuesque European deer followed me with their large, silent eyes.

The sun was already setting quickly as I began to descend the steep, circular kettle hole of No Bottom Pond. Its south slope was still snow-covered, the worn path a slick trail of ice. I began to push on consciously now; my goal was to reach the other side of the kettle hole and make a side excursion to the golf course, there to watch the woodcock's courtship display before it got too dark. The extensive bog areas to the north of the power lines here, and the numerous nearby roughs along the fairways make excellent breeding habitat for these small upland shorebirds – and a perfect spot to watch for their remarkable evening flights.

Woodcocks are not an endangered species by any means,

but their presence as a breeding bird on Cape Cod may be as more and more suitable habitat is destroyed. Already some of the roads for a new, mammoth, twelve-hundred-unit condominium project had been bulldozed in. This might be my last chance to listen to these birds here before they were replaced by other birds, the ones that one of the developers had cutely described as 'empty nesters.'

But fatigue had caught up with me and began to sap my resolve. Even as I slogged and slipped up out of the hole onto the ridge, I found my thoughts turning to food and rest, a pizza at Laurino's, perhaps even a movie in Orleans if I hurried and didn't stop to play with birds.

It had begun to turn cold, dark and windy. I looked back, dog-tired now, over the undulating hills behind me. The serpentine course of the day, marked by a linked line of electrical crosses, stretched westward back across the broken moraine toward the horizon, where a red sun, floating on its rim, now began to swim and melt.

I turned and trudged on toward the east, toward the brightening promise of lights and food, the sound of human voices . . . and then there it was, off to my right, somewhere among a young stand of pines, that unpassionate, almost comical sound that is something between a grunt and an electrical buzzer: *peent . . . peeent*. A male woodcock was warming up.

Dropping down quickly, I crouched and waited beneath the lines, the wind beginning to blow harder now, the stars starting to poke through overhead. I waited and listened. Five, ten, twelve, fifteen times the bird peented with agonizing slowness. Soon it would be too dark to see. *Come on, come on*, I urged – I'm giving up pepperoni and Woody Allen for you.

And then the dark, squat form took off, not rising in its accustomed spiral flight, but staying low, planed down by the wind, giving the whistling flight only. It banked to the east and its breast caught a last glow of russet as it swerved, the squat and long-billed form clearly visible above the trees. I stayed down on my knees, my head bent low, as the bird described a wide, low halo around me, perhaps a hundred fifty yards in diameter, swinging out over the gulf of No Bottom Pond, around to the far edge of the cleared right-of-way, then back across the wires and out over the fairway, never rising more than thirty feet, a trial flight only, finally coming to rest again into the pines where it had begun.

In a few minutes it flew again, but this time, halfway along its arc, something startled it, perhaps an involuntary movement on my part, and it flew off straight into the woods. Now the sun was gone completely. I would not hear its flight song, the woodcock's 'true' song, tonight.

But it was enough. It had provided a kind of needed benediction to the day. I stood up and walked on with all sense of haste removed, no less tired, but settled back into, and so carried on, by the rhythm of the day that I had tracked with so much effort and had nearly thrown away at the end.

Later, a full moon rose and rode along the dark tops of the pine trees, silver-washing the terrain and flooding in through swaths cut through the woods for new subdivision roads, as storm surges wash through cuts in the dunes on the Outer Beach. At intervals I heard the peents of other woodcocks along the right-of-way, responding to the moon as their ghostlike forms catapulted up into a transfigured night.

Along Millstone Road rows of new houses came right up to the power lines. Lights came on in kitchens and living rooms and I could see inside the chromatic flicker of televisions and the forms of people moving about: a woman chopping something at a counter, a family at dinner, a man petting his dog, children squatted on the floor in front of the tube.

And suddenly these familiar sights struck me as terribly strange and totally alien. These are my townspeople, I thought. Many of them I know; some are very dear to me. My ties with them are myriad and irrevocable, and without them my life would be unbearably empty. It was myself I saw through those lighted windows.

I knew that, acknowledged it, accepted it. And yet, for that moment, because of a woodcock seen briefly at sunset on a windy ridge, I stood apart and unconnected with their lives. I was a deer staring in, my head turned, slightly curious, slightly wary, but ultimately unattached and passing on.

I would go on, of course, and come at last to the lights, the food, the voices, even the movie. I would, in short, come inside where, for better or worse, human life is lived. But I kept for a long time that sense of detachment, when our lives seemed suddenly so locked in and humanly introverted, so presumptuous in our unawareness, so selective and partial even in our appreciation of that other life we call natural. I felt it would be easy and rewarding to become a perennial wanderer, a hider by day and a stalker by night, out where lives are more various and open-ended, like the spiralling, upward flight of the star-dancing woodcock.

Dawn Walk

The other night I had a rare attack of insomnia. After several attempts to overcome it, I yielded and resolved to read on into dawn. There is a strange feeling about staying up all night which I have never gotten used to, and which seems inherently unnatural. As the long hours wheel interminably on, there is a sense of gradually losing touch with the human community. One knows that the activities of men continue – that all-night parties blare on, that local police cruisers prowl the streets like cats, and invisible jets streak overhead in the velvet sky toward Europe or Boston – but they lose their universal dominance, their bravado and complacence, and dwindle to a disconnected sputtering of noise and light.

The turning point of the night passed unnoticed, and about 4 AM the whippoorwills began to sing again. The last to cease after dark, they are the first to begin in the morning. Generally speaking, the dawn serenade of birds is a reverse performance of the evening before; yet it is not an exact mirror image. The whippoorwill, for instance, does not ordinarily start his evening calls until the last of the daytime birds has quit, usually about twenty minutes after sunset. This morning, however, he was joined by a woodthrush at about 4:30 AM, and the two continued in concert together for another twenty minutes, when the whip finally ceased.

Shortly after the thrush began to sing, I stepped outside into a still, warm, muggy, clouded morning – like a bowl of soggy cereal. As I stood there, not quite sure where I was, the birds began to sing, one by one. After the thrush came the catbirds and robins, followed by phoebes, jays, towhees, starlings, song sparrows, ovenbirds and yellowthroats. There may be nothing significant or representative about this order, except that it shows that birds, like people, wake at different times.

As I came to the intersection where my dirt road meets the paved highway, the chorus was deafening. The streets were filled with song. Not even the faintest sound of a distant motor could be heard. How seldom it is during our Cape Cod summer that the sound of birdsong outweighs that of human traffic. And why do the birds sing so loudly at dawn? I had never before asked myself that obvious question; nor could I recall having read any scientific commentary on it. 'Greeting the sun' is the poet's evasion, though the sun was obscured this hazy morning. Perhaps it is their way of reminding themselves who and where they are, after a night's oblivion. We ritually read the morning paper over a muddy cup of coffee; birds sing.

I set off down the highway, the air still heavy and palpable, the darkness gradually diluting. Normally a fairly busy road in summer, it was now deserted – or rather, strangely inhabited. Catbirds, robins and towhees fed freely on the cool paved surface, casually pecking at fallen seeds or torpid insects. Faint leathery sounds whipped about my head, and I caught the fluttering indistinct forms of bats chasing late moths. A thrush flew straight at me and veered off only at the last second, as though it had not expected to see me. At one point in the road a good-sized deer stood in full view, calmly munching leaves on the other side of a stone wall. As I passed she thrust her head out over the stones to peer at me with large black eyes, as a horse will stretch its neck over a fence. Then, as though suddenly realizing what I was, she was gone, white tail flashing, ebony hooves thumping the hard ground through the underbrush.

Farther down the road, in front of a church, seven rabbits were nibbling the plantings in the empty parking lot. Nearby, oblivious to both rabbits and birds, two large cats lolled in the middle of the road like dogs at noon in a sleepy village main street. I recognized the white one with the collar; the other, a large black tom, I had never seen before. It was probably a feral, invisible by day. They turned and regarded me curiously, then looked away.

I felt, and was obviously regarded as an intruder into a landscape I had thought was familiar and hopelessly man-dominated, but which, I discovered, contained a secret society wholly unknown to daywalkers. I read somewhere that snakes are frequently seen during the early morning hours on the streets of New York City, even by sober pedestrians. Where do they disappear to during the day? Sometimes I think we do not inspire as much awe and dread in our fellow creatures as we like to think, that we are regarded more as a nuisance, to be avoided if possible, rather than as an omnipotent threat. How many of us are aware that our common thoroughfares are invaded, stalked and occupied each night and dawn by such a host of alien lives? This road possesses dimensions I did not know it had.

As I passed a small swamp I heard a familiar *quawk!* and turned to see a night heron incongruously flapping its way down the highway at head height. The early bees were already out and crowded into the smothering honeysuckle. Deerflies congregated around me, forcing me to wrap my T-shirt about my head and run on. I began to wonder if this wasn't a dream, or if humanity wouldn't somehow forget to awaken.

In the deep unity of dawn and its connected lives, the aberrations of man on the landscape seemed even more glaring than usual. Ranks of large new houses sprawled down a hillside and jostled each other for a 'waterview' of the tiny pond they surrounded. The terminal 'lollipop' of a new subdivision road slopped over its banking, the asphalt already spilling like ink down the badly eroding, unstabilized fill.

In such a time and setting the very homes of my neighbors looked strange, unfamiliar, unreal. By day they might harbor the old man-made griefs, thwarted ambition, chronic resentment, vacant boredom, silent broken marriages. Now, in the quiet of dawn, all their unseen lives seemed slight and fragile. The cars, stuffed into the driveways and lying askew, looked like toys left outside by children at bedtime. A great wave of affection and forgiveness passed through me for man and all his dubious works; I yearned to steal in and comfort their hearts.

It was the same feeling one has when looking at the loose and vulnerable form of a cross and unruly child who has slipped off into the endearing innocence of sleep. Perhaps these sleeping bodies within were also innocent, their frequently cruel acts and petty grievances – their global carelessness and blind destruction merely a mask that falls off each night – only the willful acts of children lacking constructive tasks and seeking attention in a lonely universe.

When I got back to the house, about 6:30, the spell was nearly gone. The woodthrush was still singing, but with less vigor, and the peewee, last of the morning singers, had begun. The chorus as a whole was diminished, but whatever its origins, there were good clear human-enough reasons for its breakup. For there was breakfast to be gotten, territories to be maintained, enemies to be eluded, and new lives to be fed. On the distant highway I could hear the first commuters of the morning, roaring toward Hyannis.

November Woods

 I do not know what it is about November days that makes them so likely to bring on fits of melancholy and somber moods, but they do. As one who is inordinately susceptible to the weather anyway, I am most helpless before this month. Maybe it is the final bareness that emerges behind the glory of fall, the skull behind the mask. Maybe it is just the prevalence of clouds and the tightening ring of cold around the diminishing warmth of the days, all the more noticeable here at the end of our unusually long autumns.

Whatever it is, others have noticed it. At the beginning of *Moby Dick*, Melville's hero Ishmael, describing his own melancholy and weariness of spirit, says that 'whenever it is a damp, drizzly November in my soul . . . then I account it high time to get to sea as soon as I can.' My own remedy is a little different. When soul and weather match in mood, there is nothing for it but to give in at once, to track the mood down to its source and purge it through indulgence. And for that I find more often the woods, not the sea, are best.

So, late one warm, misty afternoon last week – what Thoreau calls a 'mizzling' day – I took myself to a piece of woods I had not walked before. I knew the road where it began, and the marsh where it came out a half-mile or so beyond, but not what lay in between except that it looked somber enough for the day and me.

Just off the road, hidden in some grown-up thickets, I came on an old cellar hole; not the usual, round Cape Cod cellar, but a good-sized square one, the fieldstones carefully fitted together without mortar to a depth of five feet, deserted and overgrown, but showing no signs of caving in. A little farther on, in what was once an orchard, was an old, rotting pile of beams and boards, carefully stacked and sorted, the unframed material of some long-abandoned project.

Beyond this the woods proper began, largely open pitch pine woods, remarkably clear of briars and bushes underneath. This was evidently a pasture once and was crisscrossed with stone walls, well-made of large rocks and still in good repair thanks to the lack of heaving frosts on the Cape. The needles lay everywhere like a mat, soft and yellow-brown, and it seemed it could not have been long ago that cows wandered slowly across this gentle slope and gazed in incurious wonder at the distant sea. Now the warm November damp brought out the strong pungent smell of pine needles, and from the trees the scattered pipings of invisible tree frogs came intermittently, recalling the concentrated chorusing of the peepers in spring rains. The frogs and the drizzle and the rich pine smell gave an almost underwater atmosphere to the scene.

Further toward the marsh the land begins to drop off more rapidly into a series of small ravines and steep slopes with small terraces and dells interspersed. The stone walls had either not been built so carefully here or had fallen prey to gravity, for they had come badly apart and were tumbled down, like lines of truncated meaning. The underbrush began to increase and, as though to slow my descent, tendrils of catbriar caught at my pants. Near the remnants of the walls I noticed several groups of boulders, two and three feet across, placed together in clumps, with the sockets of earth from which they had been plucked years ago by men and oxen still visible. For what purpose had they been piled so? What unfinished dream did they represent? Who knows, who remembers now? Who, for all that, will remember or recognize our own hot projects of the day, just as obvious and necessary to their planners as these stones were to their forgotten movers? They seemed to me now like the petrified embodiments of vanished inhabitants, gathered together to hold mute counsel.

Even more deeply down the flank of the hill the stone walls and clumps were replaced by original glacial boulders ten to fifteen feet across, unmoved from where the glacier had dropped them millennia ago. Some were cleanly exposed and sat perched on the hillside as though frozen in the middle of their descent into the marsh. But most lay thickly covered and half-concealed under a layer of pine needles. They peered out at me from under shaggy brows.

Here the woods lay thicker and darkness was beginning to fall like a fine net. I felt strongly isolated, though my ears told me this was only illusion. It was easy enough to hear the roar of cars along the nearby highway. Overhead the chopping sound of a helicopter drew near, and then faded. Across the valley boomed the guns of November, blasting away after quail and pheasant in some unposted woods. It was all near enough, but it was also muted, outside of where I was.

The temptations in such scenes are far from philanthropic; but I was here to give in to temptation. What I loved about it was the sense of oldness and desertion. It seemed that no one had been in these woods for a hundred years, only the stones, like presences, brooding under the thick silence of yellowed pitch pine needles. Between two trees I saw a large rounded hump which I thought at first might be an old trash heap or woodpile. I dug into it with my hands and found under a coat of needles and loam about four inches thick, a rock surface of pink granite; it was of unusually bright color, like a bird's egg, and its surface was very rough and clean, perhaps from being eaten into by the acid of the decaying needles. It seemed ancient, more so than if it had been buried a hundred feet beneath the surface or exposed and lichen-covered on the brow of a hill.

There, in the gathering darkness, I felt that I too might live and become, like the rock, immensely old, becoming gradually covered with the detritus of living, harboring only a pink spark of consciousness, perceiving at last only faintly the muffled din of thunderstorms and the wind down the valley, and not at all the self-willed movements of men on wings and wheels.

Gannet on the Bluffs

auset Light parking lot was doing a brisk business. It was the first northeaster of the season and now, in mid-October, the lot was more crowded than it had been since Labor Day weekend. The heavy, gusty rains of the morning had temporarily ceased, but most of the storm watchers remained in their cars out of a wind that was still stiff and steady from the northeast at nearly fifty knots. A few, seeking more than spectator sport, stood at the railing along the top of the ocean bluff, smiling with a kind of open-mouthed, self-conscious excitement, as one does on a carnival ride.

For sheer power and visual spectacle, Nauset in a northeaster is better than a thousand Niagaras. Here we gather to peer over the edge of our land and watch our very foundations eroding away. At such times, the Cape itself seems no more than a low sandbar on which the ocean stumbles, momentarily, on its long, slow march toward the mainland.

I had stopped briefly here on my way out to a small beach cottage I know on the cliff road in North Eastham not far beyond Nauset Light. The cottage is built close to the edge of the ocean sand cliffs, which at that point are forty to fifty feet high. I have never met the owners, for they come here only in summer and I only in winter. But I feel, nonetheless, that I know something about them.

When I first discovered the cottage, during another northeaster nearly ten years ago, I was struck by its proximity to the cliffs and the evident erosion taking place there. I measured the distance from the seaward side of the building to the edge of the bluff that day, and I have measured it every year since. In 1971 the distance was fifty-one feet; in 1973, forty-three feet; in 1975, thirty-five feet. In 1980 it is twenty-two feet.

In other words, since I began measuring the margin of existence left to this cottage, it has lost about three and one-third feet of ground each year. This figure just happens to be almost exactly that of the estimated annual average rate of erosion for the entire Outer Beach of Cape Cod, but this is purely accidental. As anyone who has observed our outer shores for very long knows, erosion does not proceed at a uniform or equal rate. Shifting offshore bars, the severity of winter storms, currents and beach configurations, the effects of vehicular traffic on dune vegetation and many other factors all hasten or slow down the process, creating wide variation from place to place and year to year. Some beach areas are actually accreting; others, like Coast Guard Beach several miles to the south, may lose over ten feet a year.

There are any number of places along its thirty-mile stretch that provide more dramatic examples of the ocean's power, but this small cottage remains my own personal yardstick of destruction, for the effects are so immediate and on such human terms. It is one of the older cottages in the area and has probably housed several summer generations. I would guess they have been the same family, too, for the structure has a settled, cared-for look, a comfortable informality and an affectionate aversion to modernization.

Worn paths run from the house across a small yard and out to the cliff. I wonder how far these paths once ran, for they end abruptly. When I first came here there was a crude bench at the very edge, but it was gone the following autumn. Recently a protective railing has been built there, but it does not look as if it will last the coming winter.

Blasted, shrub-sized oaks and salt-seared Japanese pine grow right up to the edge, and even over, as the toppled blackened forms on the slope below me, with this year's leaves still clinging to them, showed. Peering over the brink I could see the insatiable fury of the breakers ending in patient nibbles at the base of the cliff. The fronts of the waves were quite muddy and formed a sudsy froth, intangible and dry-looking. This froth broke off from the wave edges, curled up around pieces of driftwood and then blew off down the beach like shreds of illusion. Loose lines of geese hurried south directly overhead, and a few gulls flew up like ashes from the sands.

One can plainly see that the days of this cottage are numbered. Its back is already up against the wall – that is, the cliff road – and there is no place left to go. The well-house in the yard now sits no more than ten feet from the edge of the precipice; soon it will be sucking air, or at most, salt spray. The slightly raised east windows, empty eyes of the house, can even now look down into the storm surf.

No amount of zoning regulations or 'no trespassing' signs are about to keep the sea from its own brand of development on this spot and eventual possession by an incontestable eminent domain. Surely, I thought, a diligent tax assessor would be kept busy here, adjusting his books, trying to strike a balance between increasing land values and decreasing land. And yet this cottage's family, whoever they are, will at least know its evictor well by the time the mortgage falls due in another dozen or so bittersweet years.

Carefully, I worked my way down the slope to the beach and began to walk north from the cottage, beneath the unconsolidated cliffs of the Outer Beach. Looking up, I could see the tops of the utility poles that line the cliff road. Even here, down on the beach, I heard the wind howling and whining through their wires. In places the road now swings quite close to the edge, and at one point a guy wire on one of the poles had come loose and was flapping wildly in the storm winds. The crossed poles appeared to be moving along with me, just above the trembling hairy lip of the crest. With their linked, swaying, wailing wires and a spooky yellow sun glowering, as though through frosted glass, behind them, the metaphor of a ship's masts and rigging was forceful and unavoidable.

For the next third of a mile the signs of storm damage gradually increased. Here and there along the cliff face, well casings and fiber waste pipes from former dwellings stuck up or protruded from the slope. Most of the vanished houses to which they once belonged were deserted or moved before destruction

overtook them. You will find no abandoned cellar holes on the
Outer Beach, slowly filling in and closing over with mounds of
salt-spray rose. Here a house keeps moving or it sinks swiftly out
of sight without a trace, like a vessel going down at sea.

Eventually I arrived at an area of unusually active erosion:
the scarp vegetation was sparse and ragged; rivers of sand twisted
down the banking, leaping over the more resistant outcrops of
clay and splaying out at the bottom in wide deltas; in places whole
sections of bluff twenty feet high had shelved off.

Occasionally I had to leap up the slope a few feet to avoid
a shattering slide of muddy, green surf. The tide continued
to come in, and with it came great crashing seas tumbling over
one another, carrying rafts of brown mud floating and sliding
amid milky foam. The wave volutes themselves were veined with
white vertical bands, giving them the look of curved walls of jade.

It is during 'mild' storms like this (fifty-mile-per-hour winds
or less) that beach foam seems to reach its greatest concentrations
and becomes a plaything for the mind. The upper beach was
strewn with this fluffy wreckage of the sea, scudding along in
large broken clumps like broken clouds, thrown upward in small
bits by the wind-like ashes or small panicked birds, lying on the
sands in large quivering masses flecked with innumerable tiny,
iridescent bubbles. It came slithering in, like fat muddy lips at
the edges of the waves, sliding along the wet sand on a film of its
own deliquescence, like ice melting on a hot stove. I picked up
great weightless armfuls of it, tossing it into the wind like autumn
leaves. It clung to my boots as I strode through banks of it without resistance, leaving me shod to the ankles with insubstantial
dirty snow.

Above the beach and the ocean, gray, torn banks of clouds
rushed inland with a sort of serene haste, as though their movement really had nothing to do with the palpable wind that strafed
the earth below, tearing the clinging bushes of scrub oak and
beach plum from the lips of the cliff crest. Here on this beach,
in a storm, one senses how incredibly exposed this whole land
must have been a hundred years ago when the forest cover itself
was mere rags and tatters and the gale winds, uncarded by leaf
and branch, bored down the hollows and scraped across the
rounded heaths!

I came upon one clump of blackened beach plum that had recently been torn from its moorings at the top and had slid all the way down the scarp in an upright position, following as though in sympathy the last of its impurpled leaves to the beach. Tucked down among its slender branches was a small, tightly-woven bird's nest, song sparrow's or yellowthroat's, perhaps, a touching bit of domesticity and a territory never to be returned to.

At the base of the bush were clumps of grass and dark, sandy soil that had been carried away with the roots. On the exposed underside of this turfy island I saw hundreds of small, reddish ants running about, whose nest must have been located right beneath the bush. I thought how only a short while ago they had sat (or rather scurried, for ants never sit) in subterranean security, perhaps congratulating themselves on another industrious and provisional summer, or discussing grasshoppers with tolerant condescension, when all at once, with no more warning than San Francisco will get, a chthonic catastrophe had struck. Their world had been pulled out from beneath them and within minutes they had been transported to some radically new environment.

They appeared adrift in some unfamiliar sea (as they would soon literally be), scurrying frantically over the roots and clinging soil, but not venturing out onto the unfamiliar beach. They had almost no hope or directive for scrambling back up the formidably high mountains above them. Though this scene must have occurred thousands of times previously in the history of their species on this beach, they showed no signs of having developed any behavior to cope with such disasters, any more than we would know what to do in the face of a falling moon. I felt I stood at the cutting edge of evolution, and I saw that the blade was slow and blunt.

I walked on, and a little beyond this spot the visible signs of erosion began to decrease again. Here the cliffs were about sixty feet tall, the color of bone, with horizontal bars of dark blue clay. Near the top I spotted a large grayish bird, perched sideways on one of these clay ledges. At first I thought it was an immature herring gull, but it was too large, and the head was more streamlined and tapered, like a loon's. The beak was longer, too, thinner and tightly hooked at the end. It was, I realized, an immature gannet.

I had seen these impressive, ocean-loving birds many times before. In late autumn, easterly blows often drive them close inshore or into the Bay, where they feed on small fish, twisting down in powerful dives, making cannon bursts upon the water. But I had never seen one close up. Since the clay in the cliff here afforded many handholds and ledges for climbing, it seemed a good place to make my way up and return along the cliff road.

I began slowly climbing the cliff, not attempting to conceal myself from the bird, since this was impossible, but trying at least not to startle it. It seemed to ignore me until I came quite close and could get a good look at it: a handsome goose-sized bird, with thick webbed feet, a charcoal-colored body speckled with lines of white flecks along the wings and back, a small black face mask surrounding the large eyes, and a beak like an ice pick. When I got to within a few yards of it, the gannet turned away and began to climb clumsily and laboredly up the cliff face, using its long tapered wings to row itself up. With its tail to the strong updraft, a position a bird never likes to take, its feathers were all blown backward over themselves, giving it a terribly disheveled and torn appearance.

I continued to gain on it as it climbed and flapped its way for about ten feet in this manner, when it suddenly turned and faced me, opening wide its menacing hooked beak and glaring at me with masked impersonal eyes. As it arched its wings in a threat display, I saw that some kind of fishing line was entangled in its inner right wing feathers. I glanced at my thinly gloved hands, wondering whether to risk that beak in order to catch and free the bird. Just then the gannet uttered a series of short ducklike *quawks* and rose up, swiftly, hugely, effortlessly into the updraft, hovering there a few feet above me on long, flat, tapering wings, the piece of fishing line trailing out behind it like a kite string. Then, with a slight tilt of its wings, it sailed backward up over the crest, turned, and like an arrow released from a crossbow, shot instantly out of sight.

It took me less than half a minute to scramble up the last few yards to the top of the cliff, but by then the bird was only a dark streamlined form far to the west, disappearing fast behind a grove of pitch pines. I stood there at the edge, rocking in the full force of the gale, waist-deep in dense, flattened thickets of scrub oak threaded with flapping scarlet streamers of catbriar leaves. I found myself breathing hard and trembling with that giddiness that always comes with near contact, staggering like some dazed prizefighter in the buffeting blows, as though I were being roughly punished for something I did not understand. With difficulty I made my way through the thickets and walked back south along the cliff road to where the car, rocking slowly back and forth in the wind like a tethered cow, was parked underneath whistling wires. Next to it was a car from Kansas.

That night it rained and rained. I lay in bed thinking of the gannet trailing a thin thread of fishing line over ranks of bristling pines toward the Bay. The roof gutter, its downspout choked with dead leaves, threw loud waterfalls over the edge of the eaves, and down below the house the bog at the bottom of the kettle hole slowly filled with dark water running down in trickling veins from the surrounding hills.

Winter Solstice

Late afternoon on a winter's solstice. To the west, long layers of thin purple clouds stretch and grow like coral reefs in a swimming red sea of light. Right now it seems both pleasant and important just to sit and watch the sunset slowly dissolve like this, to mark a significant moment in the year's journey and imagine I can feel the earth halt and tilt on its global hinges, and begin the slow upward climb toward summer.

It seems important to do this, because lately I have been abnormally out of touch with natural surroundings. At a recent holiday party a guest informed me that there were six feet of pack ice in Cape Cod Bay. I suddenly realized I had not been down to the shore in weeks. It made me feel as though I had been living in a foreign country, and in a sense I have. 'Pressing business' and holiday tasks have led me to spend an unusual amount of time in the confines of cities and the mazes of shopping malls. I have been wandering through wildernesses of aisles, fluorescent forests, and the sluggish deltas of checkout counters. Occasionally I passed a familiar face, but there seemed barely a moment for recognition before we were swept away on separate currents of the season's errands.

The weeks before Christmas are the time when criticism of our society's materialism reaches its height. Yet strangely enough, after one of these commercial journeys, I find that I do not feel 'materialistic,' but terribly insubstantial. In fact, I have always found it hard to think of Americans as materialists, in the sense of a people addicted to creature comforts, tangible pleasures and objects for their own sakes.

In one way, Americans are the most spiritual of peoples, if by spiritual we mean a stubborn devotion to unseen myths, promised rewards and intangible values. I do not mean by this whatever resurgence of religious heritage we may feel at this time of year, but the abstract and insubstantial nature of most of our daily lives. Our everyday view of the world, for instance, is highly charged and colored with a multitude of electronic images and public opinions – pumped in by the media and the polls – which often have little or nothing to do with our actual, sensual experience of the world.

Most of us, too, live in a financial world where our position is not based on solid, tangible assets, but on a confused and shifting series of bank accounts, bills, mortgages and a vague overriding concept called credit standing – a concept usually defined not so much by figures or dimensions but by weight, namely, the largest burden we can bear.

Not just our present, but our past seems to grow increasingly insubstantial. More and more people possess their childhoods in memory only. Not only have most of us moved away from the scenes and faces of our youth, but the places themselves have disappeared. 'They're tearing up the street where I was born,' is a motif of modern life which we have nearly completely accepted. Neighborhoods are swept away in the name of 'transportation needs,' just as forests are bulldozed off in the name of 'expanding housing pressures' – all in the name of that most elusive and unreal of all our abstract gods, 'a healthy economy.'

Cape Cod is no different. We age quickly here, too, perhaps more quickly than most places. Speaking of our towns – their populations, roads, landscape, prominent buildings and names – we tend to say, 'I remember when,' speaking of a time only one or two years gone, or less. The capacity for human change now rivals, and on the surface surpasses, natural process itself, so that the earth seems to shift under our feet. Land itself becomes little more than abstract patterns on a developer's plan or the assessor's map, coordinates for profit or taxes. We can no longer see the forest for the fees. When I pass woods and fields these days, they seem ghostlike and ephemeral, less than real.

For all I know (and what I know makes it seem likely) they are already crisscrossed with invisible lot lines and road layouts, merely waiting for a shift in the economic weather to effect their transformation into something utterly different and strange.

Not surprisingly, in the face of such encroaching insubstantiality of contemporary life, we cling to material goods and look to them for salvation from abstraction. Yet what we chase is more often the idea and not the thing itself, glittering wraiths of promises that are themselves more abstractions. We do not buy houses for comfort, fit and convenience – we buy 'good investments.' A car salesman sells us power steering, not because we need it, but because it 'undergoes little depreciation.' We buy clothes and vacations, not because we like them, but because they are 'good buys' or well-advertised.

One would think that at least in our hobbies and leisure pursuits we would seek real pleasure, but even here our choices are often guided by their therapeutic value, or because they are good exercise. As has been said many times, American accumulation of wealth and goods is not so much real as symbolic, not of financial security but of a secure sense of the material world that we so desperately lack.

Our shifting, ephemeral human world also explains, I think, our preoccupation with nature as an 'escape' from it. In the natural world we look to find a solid reality, something rooted and fixed that we can stay ourselves on. And yet, when we look closely, we find that nature is no more real than our own culture. It is, in Jacob Bronowski's phrase, 'a fugitive universe,' shifting elusive entities the essence of which, according to quantum physics, seems to be uncertainty.

I know that in these same ranks of trees I pass, whose fate seems to be up for human grabs, their seemingly solid trunks are largely an act of faith. The actual life of a tree is the merest of phantoms, a paper-thin, hollow husk of living cells, 'as delicate and transparent as a soap bubble,' as Rutherford Platt puts it. And yet these cellulose husks are continuously transforming a flow of minerals, gases and liquids into new and ingenious forms. As Rachel Carson once wrote, 'The forest borrows its materials to make temporary but emphatic statements. A tree may die, but never its idea.' I read the same lesson every time I find a cast-off crab shell, or see the ephemeral and constant flocks of butterflies each summer. It is all a sending on, both man and nature, preoccupied more with form than substance.

It is almost dark now. I look outside my window and see a bare maple, inert and dangling its limbs like a wire sculpture. But the fattened buds at the tips of the twigs hold an unseen promise, not only of a new year but of new worlds, stretching above and below sight. And I think, why should I not follow these promises more than the shaky and vacillating ones of man's own devising? I look again, and the young tree seems to shimmer and fade in the wind and the dying light, till it darkens to nothing and stars come out between its branches.

Local Gods

Over the Christmas holidays I took a non-direct flight to Louisville and found myself with an hour between planes in the airport at Pittsburgh. I had the usual choices of spending the time either (1) watching planes land and take off, (2) reading televised timetables, (3) buying a lunch I didn't really want in a restaurant decorated like an underwater cavern, (4) visiting a modernly furnished and impeccably nondenominational airport 'chapel,' or (5) watching that curious form of terminal roulette known as luggage retrieval.

I picked the first option and went up onto the observation platform to watch the planes. The airport, modern and built outside the city proper, stands atop a flattened hill, a man-made plateau, and from the observation deck I could look back toward the gray mountain ranges of the Alleghenies. All across the back of Pennsylvania there had been little snow on the ground, and from the plane those great, gray ridges, long and unbroken from north to south, had looked to my sea-conditioned eyes like the frozen crests of gigantic waves, ten miles or more in length and two thousand feet high, on an overcast, steely ocean. Now, gazing back at them from the ground, it seemed they might break, fold over and spill out onto the brown fields that lay before me.

Then I noticed that the fields were not fields at all, but a large empty golf course, spread out below the airport and within easy walking distance of it. I have always been attracted to golf courses, not for the game, but for the unexpected surprises they hold for naturalists. They represent a kind of civilized climax growth, artificially maintained, of course, but often remarkably varied and full of numerous hints of their former histories. This one, for instance, had probably once been part of the great eastern deciduous forest, which had in turn been succeeded by primitive settlements, cultivated farmland and abandoned pastureland, escaping the final fate of housing development by being preserved for community recreation.

Checking the lighted boards, I saw that my plane had been delayed once more. 'Why not?' I thought, and walked out of the terminal, dropping off the side of the plateau to have a short jaunt in an unfamiliar Pennsylvania countryside that I had been viewing, only minutes before, from a God's-eye height of twenty thousand feet. I loped off across the rolling, sloping, dead-brown fields in the rich light of a late winter afternoon. The only immediate inhabitants were a few crows, scavenging the fairways in much the same manner as they do the Cape beaches. I was evidently on the back part of the course, for there was no club-house in sight, though brick ranch houses ringed the edges.

Unconsciously, I found myself gravitating toward a large tree that stood alone in a wide ravine off the main fairway. Trees always reveal their personalities, their essential structures, much more readily in winter, and even at a distance I could see that this one bore the strong angular lines of an oak.

After several months among the stunted pines and oaks of our peninsula, I always find the size of a full-grown mainland tree startling. But this one was a giant even by inland standards. As I approached it, it seemed to grow and loom over me, weaving its branches through the slate gray sky. It was a magnificent black oak, *Quercus velutina*, rising up out of the ground like a dark, twisting, massive pillar. Its base was over six feet in diameter, and measuring it with my tape at breast height I found it to have a girth of over fourteen and a half feet.

I am not very good at estimating tree heights, but this one seemed to tower at least eighty feet into the air. The crown was not excessively wide, however, indicating that the tree started out life as part of a thick forest, spreading upward rather than out. Its outline was wonderfully dramatic, the trunk splitting early into two asymmetrical columns that leaped and soared upward in sharp, angular jumps. It had a deeply furrowed, nearly black hide, and its branches kept a surprising number of last summer's leaves, hanging in clusters like curled, coppery claws.

For all its winter 'barrenness,' it seemed to breathe life, utterly healthy, with that strong sinewy relationship that oaks possess with the earth. It was totally unlike anything the Cape had to offer, a firmly rooted, indigenous expression of these clay and limestone hills.

Without taking a core sample, I could only guess at its age, though it was certain it had flourished in this ravine for over three centuries. It had probably known bear claw, Indian knife, and the sound of settlers' axes. On one side I found the protruding end of a piece of old, rusted wire that disappeared deep into the tree's flank, the last remnant of some old fence set once to mark some now-forgotten bound or to keep contained some cows whose bones are long lost. The only other sign of man's presence, a single green metal bench already showing signs of rust and wear from the winter rains, was set next to the trunk, providing a place of rest and shade for summer golfers.

We study forest succession, the march of tree species across a landscape. But this single tree, this last local survivor of an unparalleled deciduous forest, had witnessed not only forest change, but the whole haste and ephemerality of human succession across the land. It seemed to gather the entire field to itself, to make all the fairways revolve about it, to lend a dignity to these frivolous greens and sandtraps and to justify the existence of the golf course for securing the tree's preservation.

I thought of a line from a play I saw in Boston last year: 'Life is only comprehensible in terms of a thousand local gods.' If so, here surely was one. I had been vouchsafed a glimpse of it during a stolen hour from an airport terminal, and would probably never see it again. But it impressed upon me forcibly the uniqueness, the utter irreplicatability, as definite as a human voice, of each landscape.

Here on the Cape, with its streaming seaweeds, its creeping lichens and mosses, its beach grass bent and waving in the wind, the landscape speaks to us largely in terms of acquiescence, of a kind of triumph by submission. But there, in a Pittsburgh golf course, was a commitment to a principle that admitted of no compromise with its surroundings. Life, it seemed to say, was vertical and indomitable, despite crushing odds. Life lifts itself into towers and climbs upon itself with cellulose walls and calcium girders. Life grows and reaches upward, despite the grinding, abrasive, horizontal forces of the inanimate – whether dunes, waves, glaciers, or the shoals and piles of limestone held back and in place by the tree's huge trunk.

A Day for Dead Man's Fingers

Exclusive beach rights are a cheap commodity this time of year. Though real estate prices don't dip much in winter, temperatures do. In January the Cape coasts are rarely crowded, and an 18° temperature coupled with a northwest wind of thirty-five knots will insure you nearly complete privacy and solitude at almost no expense, with free mosquito control as well.

On such a day, shortly after New Year's, I managed to make it out to the Bay – past a tangle of phone calls, conferences, children and unfinished tasks – to catch the tail end of the afternoon before it blew away completely on a hard, cold wind that had been scouring the land relentlessly since morning. I went on foot, out across Crowe's Pasture, a salt-marsh-bordered neck of land in East Dennis that had been an old pasture once but was now a conservation area largely grown up in scrub oak, scraggly cherry, beach plum and viburnum – growth appropriately stark and gaunt at this season.

I followed an old dirt road. A light covering of snow had been frozen hard for several days, but a thin dusting had settled the previous night and had recorded a single set of human tracks during the day. Not wanting to repeat recent discoveries, I left my predecessor's tracks at the first fork and continued out toward one of the handful of houses that had been built on the neck before the town rescued it for posterity.

Down below the house was the larger of two small ponds in the area, about a hundred fifty yards across and set about that far back from the beach itself. I stepped tentatively out onto its frozen surface, pausing when it snapped and cracked under my weight. But expansion cracks in the ice and bubbles underneath showed me that it was at least five inches thick. I made my way directly across the pond, toward some small dark objects that looked like dead sparrows but turned out to be goose turds. Reaching the other side, I made my way through a drying succession of pond shallows, swamp and bog, all solidly frozen and dusted lightly with snow.

The narrow band of moor and sand blowouts that now lay between me and the beach had been almost swept clean of snow by the steady wind, and it was here that I began to see how hard the freeze really was. The bare, sand slopes were as hard as concrete, and I bounced across them leaving no footprints whatsoever. The wind blew mercilessly here, slipping like a knife into the cracks and crevices of my clothing, trying to pry me open like a quahog.

The beach itself was, if anything, harder than the moors, a smooth, gradual slope barren and empty except for a few frozen slipper shells. These mollusks had been the victims of a Japanese seaweed known as *Codium fragile*, which has invaded and multiplied in our waters during the past decade, posing a serious threat to shellfish in some areas. *Codium* is aptly nicknamed 'Dead Man's Fingers,' not only for its thick, slimy, limp fronds, but because of the way it has of attaching itself to shellfish, as it had to the slipper shells, dragging them ashore on the wind and tide, and there holding onto the beach until both organisms freeze or desiccate in the burning wind.

There was also a single line of footprints on the beach ahead of me. But these had been made in another age, an ice age ago, and now lay fossilized by the cold, gathering snow dust in their dents. My own footsteps, like ghost tracks, left no prints for the spring tides to erase. Beach footprints last longest when there is pack ice in the Bay, for then the ice acts as a sea wall, keeping the tides from climbing as high as they might. If a man would leave footprints in the sands of time, let him do it in winter, just before a hard freeze.

The ice had already formed a border some thirty yards wide out in the Bay, and I could see patches of oily green slush forming beyond it at the edge of the vibrating water. Overhead, sullen wedges of Canada geese flew by, bugling metallically, and on a rock several yards out into the soft ice sat a single male eider duck – a handsome patchwork of black, white and green.

The day was getting late now, and I walked west up the beach into the teeth of the wind and a sky becoming molten gold. Further along, on a section known as Devil's Beach, the shore became strewn with large rocks and boulders, culminating in a twelve-foot-high monolith on the upper beach. I startled a small flock of black ducks that had taken refuge in its lee and took their place.

Huddled against the rock out of the buffeting wind, I watched a small flock of gulls out at the edge of the receding tide. Beyond them the Bay seethed and heaved whitecaps, a sea of wild horses. The gulls stood calm and unruffled before the fierce wind and the fury of dark water. They seem to possess a supreme nonchalance, an almost insolent indifference toward the violence of the shore, as though they were not held in the teeth of a forty-mile-per-hour gale, but were beachstrollers in June.

The nonchalance is, of course, a mask. Gulls are no more immune to the rigors of winter than other birds. I find their stiff carcasses thrown up on the beach, nonchalant no more. I have noticed, in fact, that more often than not they seem to come to more violent ends than other birds. Whether I come upon their bodies along the marshes or on the dunes or along the shore, they almost invariably lie in grotesquely contorted positions. They look like things smashed and flung down, instead of simply dead. Inland birds – sparrows, robins, and even some hawks that have succumbed to cold, hunger or disease – these I nearly always find with wings carefully folded, forming smooth, stream-lined, almost weightless packages of death that might blow across the land like leaves.

But gulls are more like the dogs, cats, raccoons and skunks one finds mashed on the highway by some passing car or truck. Their bodies are not only twisted but *driven* into the sand, matted and frozen inextricably into it. Do they die in mid-flight? Does the wind blow them awry if they turn wrong? They look as though they had been slapped down, flattened in an aerial instant by the hand of some pride-wounded divinity.

Yet these gulls, assembled in loose flocks on the lower beach, did not look as if such a fate awaited them. At least they did not seem to accept earth's harsh terms with mere abject resignation. If anything they seemed to sport with it. Casually facing the gale, one would occasionally open his wings and, without beating them, lift over the heads of his fellows and descend again. Then another would do the same, and another. There they were, ballooning lazily and gracefully over one another, using the fierce energy that planed down land and water to play leapfrog on the edge of destruction.

A hundred yards offshore, a flock of white-winged scoters beat westward into the wind, bodies stretched out, keeping low in the green troughs of the waves, wings beating rhythmically and in unison with intense purpose and great effort. 'Keep close, keep together,' they seemed to say, as though life were a matter of grim discipline. The hard lines of the day did not contradict them. Everything seemed to press life down into lower and lower profiles.

On the western horizon one of the Cape's violent winter sunsets began to play itself out. Above the serrated turbulence of the waterline, the air itself became visible and shimmered horizontally with wind and cold, much as it rises in vertical waves off a hot pavement in summer. To the north clouds were breaking up, tinted incongruously with soft pastel shades of blue and pink.

It was intensely lovely to watch, but the beach and stones had an unnerving, pre-human aspect, and it was not just the cold that forced me to move again before the show was over. I climbed the bluff and walked among a string of empty summer cottages, boarded blind for the winter. If I had looked a little more closely I might have seen the foundations themselves weathering. I could easily have believed that men had left for good, and that I was only a relict or guardian spirit looking on, if the biting wind had not kept reminding me of my flesh-and-blood reality.

Heading inland again, I did meet one man, a hunter, a figure clad wholly in white – white jacket, white pants, white gloves, white hood – invisible against the snow until he emerged suddenly quite near, startling me. So inhuman he looked, not an inch of flesh showing, that for a brief moment I wondered if he might be out for me, the last of my kind. But he was after other game, rabbit or pheasant, and with a brief nod from behind silvered ski glasses, he passed silently and harmlessly by.

I made my way quickly back across the frozen pond, sliding before the wind, the ice whooping and cracking behind me as though reprimanding me for such childish fancies – then up the hill and back down the dirt road through a dead landscape bathed in light like blood. A nearby church bell clanged five o'clock like a warning.

When I returned home my wife asked me where I had been. I was hard put to say. 'On the beach' hardly seemed adequate. I felt that I had gone farther and been gone longer, and that there was some nagging meaning to the whole strange excursion that I could not quite grasp. Yet there seemed nothing definite I had learned or discovered from it – unless it was how willing the imagination is to indulge itself in trying to fill up such an empty and whitened world.

An Assault of Grackles

This week, as they have every fall since we moved here, the grackles have settled in around our house, flashing through the woods in loose black nets, like thieves of summer. Usually they arrive in company with other birds, sometimes as early as mid-August with migrating young robins, more often early in September with redwings, cowbirds and starlings, but in other years not till mid-month, coming in with the first flocks of white-crowned sparrows, or even later, showing up with the first juncos of October.

With whomever and whenever the grackles arrive, the difference is that they stay. After the robins, the other blackbirds and the sparrows have moved on, I open the door in the morning and find them there: large, black, iridescent birds with bright yellow eyes and long, curved bills, balanced by long, keel-shaped tails – feeding under the tupelo grove. As I step outside they fly up with a rustling flutter of wings, leisurely, with strong crow-like beats, calling to one another with sharp *chip*s and high rusty *squee-ee*s as they disperse into the woods.

Grackles are not all that common as fall migrants over most of the Cape. Flocks of a hundred or more have been counted on the Outer Cape, and four hundred plus were once sighted in Bourne near the Canal, but nothing like the concentrations of a half-million or more that sometimes move in dark blanketing clouds, with the sound of a vast electrical storm, through the Connecticut River Valley.

Still, my house seems to be in the path of a minor but regular flyway, and in some years I have counted over two hundred birds moving through the woods. I suspect this is due in part to the sixty acres of nearly pure oak that surround our lot. Acorns form one of the major autumn food sources for the grackles, which crack the hard shells by direct pressure of their strong bills. It is probably the abundance of nuts in our woods at this time of year and the presence of a nearby swamp that make them pause here on their erratic but inexorable movement south.

At any rate, they have become a regular local sign of autumn and linger long enough for me to have gotten some sense of their habits and character. They come closest to the house in early morning when, wakening from sleep, I hear their noisy chatter in the oak branches, a sound like tons of scrap metal pouring down a metal chute. They are most active then, crashing through the trees and catbriar thickets, stabbing at bark insects, tearing off acorns and shadberries, ushering in the day with a sound of violence.

Later in the morning they tend to move around and feed under the tupelos in front of the house with the sparrows and the chipmunks. By midday they usually disappear, roosting quietly somewhere in the woods at a distance from us. One afternoon in early October I came upon a flock of sixty or seventy birds near the bog at the bottom of the wooded slope in back of the house. Most were invisible, down on the forest floor searching for insects in the wet leaves like a horde of towhees. Others perched in the shrubs and lower branches, pecking away at dead limbs. All around me I heard a general rustling sound as hundreds of dark feet shuffled through the fallen leaves and tapped on dead wood. Yet by late afternoon they were back in the tops of the oaks circling the house, calling loudly, energetically, aggressively to one another, plucking acorns off the branches, many of which dropped and bounced off the roof with loud *thocks* or hit the ground with heavy *plops*.

So they shuttle back and forth around our house over a period of two, three, or as many as five weeks, but always with a net drift south, carried along the crests of the oaks like black flotsam of the season.

I have been trying, while writing this, to think of a word that describes my feeling about these grackles. The closest I can come seems to be 'alien,' though I don't know why this should be. Grackles are as native as chickadees and hardly to be equated with such foreign interlopers as starlings and weaver finches. Perhaps it is because, like herring gulls, they are native birds unnaturally prevalent. Originally marsh birds of forested regions, their range and numbers expanded enormously as they took advantage of the grain fields provided by early settlers.

Today grackles still have bad press among farmers, but the damage they do in their fields is probably more than balanced by their role in controlling such crop pests as cornborers and cutworms. Even around suburban lawns and gardens they perform beneficial services, eating much weed seed and Japanese beetles, and feeding prodigious numbers of insect grubs to their insatiable young.

Grackles are also one of the few native birds that have been able to hold their own against the encroaching competition from starlings and English sparrows, though this is no great improvement in many people's eyes. Still, they have never taken any of *my* corn, nor do they seem to frighten other birds away from the house.

I have to confess, however, to a persistent feeling of, if not enmity, at least apprehension regarding them. I cannot really account for it rationally, or even aesthetically. The grackle is an intelligent, adaptable bird, strong of wing, glistening in his nuptial iridescent plumage, possessing a certain beauty of movement like a ship in flight. He has none of the ragtag malignancy of the starling about him. His stare is cold, yes, but it is a coldness of reserve and nobility rather than evil.

Their calls and thrashings disturb my dreams at dawn, but that is not enough to account for the curious and unexpected sense of dread I sometimes get when I open the door and come upon them, bent over and feeding in the yard. To be sure, they take off at my approach, but there is (or seems to be) a split second of hesitation before they do, as though they had to *remind* themselves to be afraid of me.

As far as I know, grackles carry no folk connotations of doom with them, though blackbirds in general, and ravens in particular, have figured as symbols of death in western literature for centuries. Their sudden expansion of range and numbers with the coming of agriculture can give one pause, though, as yet another indication that other species are not mere fixed, passive entities, waiting to be destroyed or preserved by man, but are, like us, vessels of combustible genetic energy, waiting only for some environmental change to be released and fly off in bold new directions.

However true this may be, it still does not account for my own reaction to these birds. I am not a superstitious person by nature. The sudden, epiphanic appearances of snakes, hawks or deathwatch beetles may alter my moods, but not my expectations about life.

The arrival of the grackles, on the other hand, can throw an inexplicable pall over what is otherwise an exhilarating, upbeat season. One year, during the week they arrived, a boat that I was watching for a neighbor was stolen from its mooring in the Bay, a good friend was rushed to the hospital with a heart attack, and on the Mid-Cape Highway I hit a deer, breaking its back.

Last year on Labor Day, my son, out riding his bike, fell and broke his collarbone, sending us all to the emergency room for most of the day. The following day, Tuesday, the car would not start, for reasons unfathomable even to the mechanic who came out to look at it. On Wednesday the cat disappeared and the resin I had spread on our new deck refused to dry. On Thursday the pump broke. That afternoon my wife and I quarreled violently, for no good reason. And on Friday, as the Red Sox were giving up first place for good by dropping their fourth straight to New York, I cut my knuckle on the table saw, taking seven stitches. My fortunes seemed, like those of the Sox, subject to sudden, unpredictable fluctuations and wholesale slumps. And then, on Saturday morning, I was wakened out of a troubled sleep by the sound of grackles thrashing through the oaks, dark images blurred and distorted through streaks of rain that ran like tears on the window glass.

The following week the cat came back, the car started, we bought a new pump, and shoulder, knuckle and all other wounds eventually healed. Boston even managed a moment of near glory in Fenway Park at the end of the month. But what had been only a vague feeling of apprehension had crystallized into something definite and permanent, if not wholly justifiable. As I say, I am not superstitious. I infer no design, suggest no malice, draw no conclusions. I merely state the juxtapositions and assert that certain things gain meanings merely by association that are as strong as any produced by logical cause and effect.

This week there is an autumn chill in the air. The blueberries are gone as though they never were, and in the woods mushrooms have replaced the ladyslippers of May. A few bruised, purple beach plums still dangle on their stems, blue asters bloom coolly by the roadsides, and the light is once again noticeably slanted. At work my typewriter refuses to advance its ribbon and, as I drive home, the muffler goes. On the radio men seem more intent than ever on destroying what is beautiful and valuable. Violence is up in Boston. There is a chance of frost predicted for Vermont tonight.

At five o'clock I pull into the drive. The grackles are there. I hear them high in the trees. I am not surprised. I start up the path to the house – not quite running, but holding a book over my head as a shield against the bombardment of acorns that drop from their beaks.

A Civil Death

Like so many others, I have all but abandoned the romance of an open wood fire for the more efficient, if more prosaic, heat of an airtight stove. Unlike many, however, my stove has its own separate flue, so that the hearth is still available for guests and holidays, taking the place of caviar and champagne. On New Year's Eve some pop a cork. We strike a match.

By late spring, however, when the stove begins to sit cold for days at a time and the wood supply is running low, I usually treat myself to a few last extravagant fires in the evening, the way a man will sometimes blow his last ten dollars of the month on a steak. My fires are more like soybean hamburgers, however, for what I usually have left by then are soggy, half-rotted, dead limbs gleaned from the spring woods.

Whenever one stores wood inside for any length of time before burning it, there is a good chance of releasing insects into the house. This is particularly true of dead wood or wood that has been left outside to age through an entire summer. Last summer we had in our kitchen an infestation of strange worms, which even the county entomologist could not identify. I suspect they immigrated inside a log.

One day last February, after splitting some old pitch pine, I brought in some logs. The bark had fallen off during the chopping, and their outer surfaces were decorated with the elaborate radiating patterns of bark beetle larvae as well as numerous little oval depressions about three-eighths of an inch long. In each depression a larva had hatched and bored itself out of a little nest, piling up the shredded wood around and over itself. Most of the nests were empty, but I found a few curled, segmented grubs that were covered with white ice crystals and appeared utterly frozen. Yet later that evening, as I was about to put one of these logs into the stove, a small, brown, mothlike creature emerged from one of the nests. Leaving its empty shell behind, the insect crawled out onto the end of the log where it fluttered off on drab wings up into the thin night of the ceiling beams.

Last Saturday night I stayed up late reading. The rest of the family had gone to bed. For company I built a fire in the fireplace, the first one in months. The damp wood took some coaxing and blowing but finally caught, and I sat happily beside it absorbed in my book while it sputtered and wheezed like an old asthmatic dog.

After a while I looked up and saw a group of small insects crawling around on the end of the log nearest me. They were ants. Undoubtedly they had made their winter home inside this piece of rotten wood and had now been evicted from it by the heat of the fire. For a few minutes the ants mulled about on the end of the log, which leaned up against a large stone I was using as a hob for the teakettle. I wondered why they did not simply crawl down over the stone and across the hearth to safety. Then I realized that the fire, which had been burning for some time, had heated the stone enough to keep the kettle steaming. The ants were trapped with no negotiable way out.

What struck me about their plight was that they did not panic and scatter as, say, sowbugs or people might have done in a similar situation. In fact, while remaining in almost constant motion, the ants nevertheless stayed calm and orderly. They continually touched each other's antennae, communicating, literally scratching one another's heads to find some way out. I think it was this apparent calmness in the face of disaster that initially restrained me from helping them out of their jam. Industrious and resourceful creatures that they are, they had me convinced they would find a solution, and I was coldly curious to see what it might be.

One individual crawled into a crevice at the end of the log, but a moment later it scuttled back out just ahead of a spurt of steam. Immediately the ant ran back and began vigorously touching antennae with its fellows, as though saying, 'No way out there!'

After that the ants, about thirty or so, remained together, occasionally running to and fro on hairlike, hunched-up legs, but gradually massing into a tighter and tighter group. Still they showed no sign of panic, unless there was a hint of increased rapidity in their uninterrupted antennae touching as they continued to discuss the situation, repeatedly, interminably, committee-like, while the fire gradually consumed the log.

In the end it was not flame but water that drove them off. The heat of the fire continued to push the internal moisture out the end of the log. It darkened the end-grain of the wood with a thick bubbling mixture, spitting and spewing steam and hot gobbets of sap back onto the gathered ants. I stood hypnotized, fascinated, as incapable of action as if the fire had been a television screen showing me a disaster movie rather than a true-life drama.

Ministers, sociologists and talk-show hosts endlessly discuss the 'non-involvement' of modern man: of citizens who pass by crimes being committed in broad daylight, of neighbors who resolutely ignore the cries of victims they know being stabbed to death in the night, of pilots who burn and bomb entire villages and their inhabitants while chatting about basketball scores. Too easily, I think, we chalk up such phenomena to cowardice or cultural narcissism or (that great catch-all phrase of our century) 'alienation.' Ants, it is true, may exist on the outer edges of human sympathy. But their plight and my reaction to it made me wonder if our noninvolvement, or at least a part of it, is the result of a carefully nurtured consumer mentality for which television has been the most effective evangelist, though by no means the only one. Have we been trained, in other words, to feel that life and death are things to be observed and consumed, rather than to be participated in?

At last one of the ants cracked. As though flung off a pinwheel, it broke violently from the group, racing off the log and down onto the glowing coals. A moment later I heard its small, hard body crackle. Then a few more took off, almost in spite of themselves, down across the hob stone. They had been right at first. The stone proved hot beyond their endurance, and they crumpled up and sizzled into black specks of soot halfway across its dry, deadly surface. Others panicked and followed the first ant directly down into the heart of the inferno. Where, I wondered, was blue-eyed Paul Newman, putting out the fire, escaping the volcano, saving the children?

Yet, though panicked, they still moved with admirable deliberateness, as though they had decided, 'It's hopeless – let's end it fast.' Even to the end a small stable core remained intact, a body of concerned citizens of a complex insect society rooted in natural law and order, capable of amazing feats of engineering and organization. Even as the flames drew nearer they continued to talk and discuss with one another, touching antennae as though in more communication and more information lay salvation itself. Even as the searing heat finally curled and crinkled their antennae, riving forever all further communication, they seemed to continue thinking in blind isolation and growing darkness of the flame, continuing to believe, even as it engulfed them, that there must, *must* be some civil and orderly way out of this.

A Moth in the Eye

The other evening I was sitting under a lamp doing some research on the migration schedules of our local shorebirds. I was holding in my lap a large book filled with beautiful, soft watercolors of these graceful birds, when rather suddenly several moths began leaping and fluttering across its broad pages – moths with polished, burnished wings, rigid deltoids with elaborate black-and-white filigree on their backs; moths with smooth antennae, curled antennae, feathery antennae; moths with proboscises coiled downward like clock springs or thrown back over their heads like raised elephant trunks; moths with incredibly elastic front legs – all darting, flitting, jumping, all saying, 'Look here, look at me,' until one flew into my eye and I had to put the book down.

We need to look more at insects, if only to recognize them for what they are. We avoid them so deliberately that I doubt if many adults could give a reasonably accurate, objective description of the commonest garden bugs we spend so much time trying to get rid of. Even in our pesticide ads they are depicted as cartoon characters, anatomically absurd and with faces either childishly monstrous or likeably misguided, but nothing whatsoever like the real things.

Every summer night, attracted by the hall light, a host of moths and other flying insects crowd their pale bodies against the black windows of my front door. The bugs and smaller moths butt and bump softly, silently against the panes, bouncing away again. The mosquitoes flatten their proboscises, or sucking tubes, against the glass, while the larger moths just hang there motionlessly, like dead kites, staring in with their dark, blind eyes.

It is a most gentle siege, a passive threat – hardly something to get anxious about. There is no real aggression in their crowding, of course; if they had serious intentions, they could manage to crawl in around the jamb or under the threshold.

Ordinarily, we see moths only around lights, when they are unnaturally disoriented, inept and awkward in their trapped flight. How does a moth fly in darkness? There is surprisingly little written about the flying equipment of these insects. One source suggests that they navigate using the stars and moon as reference points, and that the brighter, artificial lights throw them off the beam. Whatever the cause of their attraction to lights, moths evolved long ago in prehuman darkness where the disruptive effects of man-made illumination did not exist. Its presence is so recent that the moths have had no time to evolve an adaptation to it. And as we push the darkness further and further back with our lights, moths become increasingly our insect satellites, ringing our fluorescent, incandescent and mercury vapor beacons with their soft, fat, furry, muffling bodies.

They hang and bump and press with the patient indifference of water dripping on stone. It is not so much that they are *trying* to get in that strikes me, but that they *would be everywhere* if they could. They press with a tendency too vague to be resisted, a force too dispersed to be opposed.

One night earlier this summer I came home from a special town meeting, one that lasted long and was full of much heat and sweeping statements – you may know the kind. When I reached the front door, I found the moths there, blocking my way. To avoid letting in a cloud of insects, I had to sneak around the house and come in the unlit back door. When I was inside, the importance and significance of the evening's doings, in which I had been caught up and in which so much seemed to be decided or disposed of, dwindled to nothing. The moths had made me realize that we are like children, like very small children who do not yet understand that the world is not just an extension of ourselves. Caught up in our own concerns, we fail to see the world that is distinct from us – a world with its own lives, aims and desires. Like infants we tend to treat it as though it were actually a part of us, that is, as though its inherent potential were solely to conform to our own desires.

We decree a direction for nature and provoke it with blind reachings out and crude tamperings; and when it does not conform, when it strikes out on its own path, we blame the world's perverseness and redouble our heavy-handed tactics. (Or, like somewhat older children, we blame our fellow nations.)

The difference in the analogy is, of course, that while nature does give each of her children a reasonable chance for survival, she is not a tolerant, indulgent, protective or even constructively disciplinary parent. She doesn't care. It doesn't care. The moths at my door are totally indifferent to me, to town budgets, to proposed golf courses and new police cruisers. They are, in fact, indifferent to their own fate; a moth's existence cannot possibly matter to anyone but a human being.

This is why I think moths and other insects are so important. Their indifference to themselves and to us and both our fates is so complete and total that we dare not see them for what they are. We must caricature them as malicious and designing ('nature on the rampage') so that we do not recognize the terrible impartiality of their existence, their total unawareness of our own. More than any other form of higher life, insects seem at home in an indifferent universe.

As we seek to dominate the earth, we find more and more that we can do so only by destroying it. And as we succeed, we become masters of an increasingly barren world. But it would be a mistake to think that the rest of nature cowers abjectly in ever-shrinking recesses and dark corners of a man-dominated world, waiting there in passive acceptance for us to deliver either the final coup de grâce or a humanitarian reprieve.

Nothing on earth ever accepts defeat in that sense except man. As the woods go and the bulldozers arrive, I know that the woodcocks will continue to rise in starry parabolas on soft spring nights, that box turtles will nudge onward toward slow matings in the deep moist grass beneath the locusts, and that the moths – the moths will go on bumping ceaselessly, softly, patiently against glowing detours, whose origins or length of duration they cannot care about, until the last human light goes out forever.

Old School Pictures

Until a year ago my son's Cub Scout pack held its monthly meetings in the basement gymnasium of the old elementary school. This past fall our new school was opened and the pack now meets in the new cafeteria, a much more cheerful and better-lighted place for the meetings. In fact, there is only one thing I miss about the old basement, and I would like very much to find out what has become of it.

Along one side of its pine-paneled walls there was hung a long row of old school pictures, some dating back to the late 1800s. Sometimes during the entertainment portions of the meetings (which were geared for the boys and not for their parents), I would amuse myself by drifting over to these pictures and examining them, taking each one down in turn in its funny, old-fashioned frame, and then replacing it carefully on its nail.

My favorite picture was the oldest one, dated 1888, of 'District School No. 5,' located in the southern part of our town. It showed a small, simple, woodframe building, gable-fronted, standing in the middle of a flat, treeless plain. In front of the building a small group of perhaps fifteen children was lined up with their teacher. Their heights varied from barely three to over five feet. They all looked uncomfortable, in clothes either too big or too small for them, the girls in heavy calico dresses, the boys in tight-fitting pants and jackets buttoned to the neck.

The smallest child of all was a tiny thing on the left end, whose features were shadowed by a large sunbonnet (like the old, faceless Dutch Cleanser girl). Her name was listed as Bernice Small.

The teacher, only slightly taller than the tallest boy, was identified as a Miss Palmer. She looked young and fairly handsome, and was shown staring firmly off to one side. Virtually all the names inked in underneath the picture were old ones to the area: Ellis, Howe, Baker, Small. There were others — Maker, Briggs, Bearse — which have not survived so well down to the present day, except in some of the newer subdivision and street names.

These old pictures grabbed me so, I could not account for it. It was not just the quaintness of dress and the radically different landscape. These little figures looked so vulnerable, so fragile out on that barren windswept plain, with only the firm jaw of their teacher to sustain them. Today we are apt to think of our relationship to this planet in terms of a technological death grip, but these children suggested the real isolation of the human spirit in the cosmos and made me feel that no advantage they might have managed to scrape up against it would have seemed unfair (even though, in this case, the visual wilderness was of their own, or rather, their fathers' making). I loved them, among other things, for their total, incomprehensible unawareness of me.

By 1895, some of the 'new-old' names began to appear in the pictures: Gage, Tubman, Dugan, Alexander — many of whose descendants still live in the town. Most of the pictures over the next three decades were taken at the old school in the center of town, now a plastics factory. The earliest names I know personally appeared in 1909, those of two women who still live near me. A 1916 picture shows both of them sitting in adjacent rows at their dark, wooden desks, bows in their flat, straight hair. I looked hard to see the older women in the schoolgirl faces, and it seemed that already their basic outlooks on the world had formed: one already somewhat dour, apprehensive and resentful of the world, and tending to plumpness; the other, thinner and with a less determined face, not as strong in character but more hopeful and trusting of the world.

As children they played together in the cemetery next door where my children sometimes play now. Both later married, one to a local boy shown in the school pictures with her, the other to an off-Cape man. Now they both live as widows, a half-mile apart, in the old family homes they grew up in, divested of husbands and other external trappings, returned to home. Although I have lived here only a few years and my own parents had not yet been born when these women went to grade school, their pictures made me feel strangely old, for I realized that I was one of a small number of the present townspeople who still knew them.

Only in the late twenties and thirties did many faces begin to appear that I know now, men still in their prime, some of whom hold town positions or are prominent tradesmen, who went to school here in that period when all boys seemed to be very gangly and had curly hair.

From about 1938 to 1955 there was a gap, when no pictures appeared. When they began again, in the late fifties, they were no longer of entire schools, but of individual grades. A daughter of my neighbor appeared briefly, in 1958, showing her father's lineaments. From then on, the names of the students began to change and diversify much more rapidly, as though a slow-motion film were accelerating to time-lapse speed. Still, as late as the graduating class of 1971 (the last eighth grade to go to school in our local grade school), fully a third of the twenty-four names were still those of old families.

A friend of mine once told me that he had outgrown his interest in local history during his years here. I find my own tendency just the reverse: the longer I live here the more I find myself preoccupied with things that were. Part of it is that, the more closely I look at the natural landscape, the more it seems involved with our human past. Part of it is also, I know, the desire we all have to rescue temporal things from oblivion. In the lists of names below the older pictures there were frequently blank spaces between commas. These struck me painfully, for I could not even give the corresponding anonymous faces an identity.

But I think I valued these pictures not just as symbols of a lost past, or as factors in our land-use history, but as a perspective on the present. The children in them are largely invisible now, covered up like the timbers in old houses that have passed into new hands and been remodeled. In recent decades a pattern of new names (mine among them) has pasted itself across the face of this town. Yet in time the glue of our opportunism will loosen and we will peel off like cheap wallpaper.

In the old pictures the foreign names of the teachers – Palmer, Le Fort, Dunn – come and pass away with each new photograph, but the small children remain like kingposts. Today we still travel their roads, walk their beaches and endure their seasons. We have 'conquered' space and mistake it for time, while in their guileless, unguarded faces I read the intent to strike roots deep into the void.

(Behind me, I heard the voices of the Cub Scouts sitting on the old gymnasium floor, and my attention was drawn away from the pictures. They were laughing at an old film of Lindbergh's epic flight, already comic in its antiquity.)

Very Like a Whale

One day last week at sunset I went back to Corporation Beach in Dennis to see what traces, if any, might be left of the great, dead finback whale that had washed up there several weeks before. The beach was not as hospitable as it had been that sunny Saturday morning after Thanksgiving when thousands of us streamed over the sand to gaze and look. A few cars were parked in the lot, but these kept their inhabitants. Bundled up against a sharp wind, I set off along the twelve-foot swath of trampled beach grass, a raw highway made in a few hours by ten thousand feet that day.

I came to the spot where the whale had beached and marveled that such a magnitude of flesh could have been there one day and gone the next. But the carcass had been hauled off and the tide had smoothed and licked clean whatever vestiges had remained. The cold, salt wind had lifted from the sands the last trace of that pervasive stench of decay that clung to our clothes for days, and now blew clean and sharp into my nostrils.

The only sign that anything unusual had been there was that the beach was a little too clean, not quite so pebbly and littered as the surrounding areas, as the grass above a new grave is always fresher and greener. What had so manifestly occupied this space a short while ago was now utterly gone. And yet the whale still lay heavily on my mind; a question lingered, like a persistent odor in the air. And its dark shape, though now sunken somewhere beneath the waves, still loomed before me, beckoning, asking something.

What was it? What had we seen? Even the several thousand of us that managed to get down to the beach before it was closed off did not see much. Whales, dead or alive, are protected these days under the Federal Marine Mammals Act, and shortly after we arrived, local police kept anyone from actually touching the whale. I could hardly regret this, since in the past beached whales, still alive, have had cigarettes put out in their eyes and bits of flesh hacked off with pocket knives by souvenir seekers. And so, kept at a distance, we looked on while the specialists worked, white-coated, plastic-gloved autopsists from the New England Aquarium, hacking open the thick hide with carving knives and plumbing its depths for samples to be shipped to Canada for analysis and determination of causes of death. What was it they were pulling out? What fetid mystery would they pluck from that huge coffin of dead flesh? We would have to trust them for the answer.

But as the crowds continued to grow around the whale's body like flies around carrion, the question seemed to me, and still seems, not so much why did the whale die, as why had we come to see it? What made this dark bulk such a human magnet, spilling us over onto private lawns and fields? I watched electricians and oil truck drivers pulling their vehicles off the road and clambering down to the beach. Women in high heels and pearls, on their way to Filene's, stumbled through the loose sand to gaze at a corpse. The normal human pattern was broken and a carnival atmosphere was created, appropriate enough in the literal sense of 'a farewell to the flesh.' But there was also a sense of pilgrimage in those trekking across the beach, an obligation to view such a thing. But for what? Are we really such novices to death? Or so reverent toward it?

I could understand my own semiprofessional interest in the whale, but what had drawn these hordes? There are some obvious answers, of course: a break in the dull routine, 'something different.' An old human desire to associate ourselves with great and extraordinary events. We placed children and sweethearts in front of the corpse and clicked cameras. 'Ruthie and the whale.' 'Having a whale of a time on Cape Cod.'

Curiosity, the simplest answer, doesn't really answer

anything. What, after all, did we learn by being there? We were more like children at a zoo, pointing and poking, or Indians on a pristine beach, gazing in innocent wonder at strange European ships come ashore. Yet, as the biologists looted it with vials and plastic bags and the press captured it on film, the spectators also tried to *make* something of the whale. Circling around it as though for some hold on its slippery bulk, we grappled it with metaphors, lashed similes around its immense girth. It lay upside down, overturned 'like a trailer truck.' Its black skin was cracked and peeling, red underneath, 'like a used tire.' The distended, corrugated lower jaw, 'a giant accordian,' was afloat with the gas of putrifaction and, when pushed, oscillated slowly 'like an enormous waterbed.' Like our primitive ancestors, we still tend to make images to try to comprehend the unknown.

But what were we looking at? Or more to the point, from what perspective were we looking at it? What did we see in it that might tell us why we had come? A male finback whale – *Balaenoptera physalus* – a baleen cetacean. The second largest creature ever to live on earth. An intelligent and complex mammal. A cause for conservationists. A remarkably adapted swimming and eating machine. Perfume, pet food, engineering oil. A magnificent scientific specimen. A tourist attraction. A media event, a 'day to remember.' A health menace, a 'possible carrier of a communicable disease.' A municipal headache and a navigational hazard. Material for an essay.

On the whale's own hide seemed to be written its life history, which we could remark but not read. The right fluke was almost entirely gone, lost in some distant accident or battle and now healed over with a white scar. The red eye, unexpectedly small and mammalian, gazed out at us with fiery blankness. Like the glacial scratches sometimes found on our boulders, there were strange marks or grooves in the skin around the anal area, perhaps caused by scraping the ocean bottom.

Yet we could not seem to scratch its surface. The whale – dead, immobile, in full view – nonetheless shifted kaleidoscopically before our eyes. The following morning it was gone, efficiently and sanitarily removed, like the week's garbage. What was it we saw? I have a theory, though probably (as they say in New England) it hardly does.

There is a tendency these days to defend whales and other endangered animals by pointing out their similarities to human beings. Cetaceans, we are told, are very intelligent. They possess a highly complex language and have developed sophisticated communications systems that transmit over long distances. They form family groups, develop social structures and personal relationships, and express loyalty and affection toward one another. Much of their behavior seems to be recreational: they sing, they play. And so on.

These are not sentimental claims. Whales apparently do these things, at least as far as our sketchy information about their habits warrants such interpretations. And for my money, any argument that helps to preserve these magnificent creatures can't be all bad.

I take exception to this approach not because it is wrong, but because it is wrongheaded and misleading. It is exclusive, anthropocentric, and does not recognize nature in its own right. It implies that whales and other creatures have value only insofar as they reflect man himself and conform to his ideas of beauty and achievement. This attitude is not really far removed from that of the whalers themselves. To consume whales solely for their nourishment of human values is only a step from consuming them for meat and corset staves. It is not only presumptuous and patronizing, but it is misleading and does both whales and men a grave disservice. Whales have an inalienable right to exist, not because they resemble man *or* because they are useful to him, but simply because they do exist, because they have a proven fitness to the exactitudes of being on a global scale matched by few other species. If they deserve our admiration and respect, it is because, as Henry Beston put it, 'They are other nations, caught with ourselves in the net of life and time, fellow prisoners of the splendour and travail of life.'

But that still doesn't explain the throngs who came pell-mell to stare and conjecture at the dead whale that washed up at Corporation Beach and dominated it for a day like some extravagant *memento mori*. Surely we were not flattering ourselves, consciously or unconsciously, with any human comparisons to that rotting hulk. Nor was there much, in its degenerate state, that it had to teach us. And yet we came – why?

The answer may be so obvious that we have ceased to recognize it. Man, I believe, has a crying need to confront otherness in the universe. Call it nature, wilderness, the 'great outdoors,' or what you will – we crave to look out and behold something other than our own human faces staring back at us, expectantly and increasingly frustrated. What the human spirit wants, as Robert Frost said, 'Is not its own love back in copy-speech, / But counter-love, original response.'

This sense of otherness is, I feel, as necessary a requirement to our personalities as food and warmth are to our bodies. Just as an individual, cut off from human contact and stimulation, may atrophy and die of loneliness and neglect, so mankind is today in a similar, though more subtle, danger of cutting himself off from the natural world he shares with all creatures. If our physical survival depends upon our devising a proper use of earth's materials and produce, our growth as a species depends equally upon our establishing a vital and generative relationship with what surrounds us.

We need plants, animals, weather, unfettered shores and unbroken woodland, not merely for a stable and healthy environment, but as an antidote to introversion, a preventive against human inbreeding. Here in particular, in the splendor of natural life, we have an extraordinary reservoir of the Cape's untapped possibilities and modes of being, ways of experiencing life, of knowing wind and wave. After all, how many neighborhoods have whales wash up in their backyards? To confine this world in zoos or in exclusively human terms does injustice not only to nature, but to ourselves as well.

Ever since his beginnings, when primitive man adopted totems and animal spirits to himself and assumed their shapes in ritual dance, *Homo sapiens* has been a superbly imitative animal. He has looked out across the fields and seen and learned. Somewhere along the line, though, he decided that nature was his enemy, not his ally, and needed to be confined and controlled. He abstracted nature and lost sight of it. Only now are we slowly realizing that nature can be confined only by narrowing our own concepts of it, which in turn narrows us. That is why we came to see the whale.

We substitute human myth for natural reality and wonder why we starve for nourishment. 'Your Cape' becomes 'your Mall,' as the local radio jingle has it. Thoreau's 'huge and real Cape Cod . . . a wild, rank place with no flattery in it,' becomes the Chamber of Commerce's 'Rural Seaside Charm'—until forty tons of dead flesh wash ashore and give the lie to such thin, flattering conceptions, flesh whose stench is still the stench of life that stirs us to reaction and response. That is why we came to see the whale. Its mute, immobile bulk represented that ultimate, unknowable otherness that we both seek and recoil from, and shouted at us louder than the policeman's bullhorn that the universe is fraught, not merely with response or indifference, but incarnate assertion.

Later that day the Dennis Board of Health declared the whale carcass to be a 'health menace' and warned us off the beach. A health menace? More likely an intoxicating, if strong, medicine that might literally bring us to our senses.

But if those of us in the crowd failed to grasp the whale that day, others did not have much better luck. Even in death the whale escaped us: the tissue samples taken in the autopsy proved insufficient for analysis and the biologists concluded, 'We will never know why the whale died.' The carcass, being towed tail-first by a Coast Guard cutter for a final dumping beyond Provincetown, snapped a six-inch hawser. Eluding further attempts to reattach it, it finally sank from sight. Even our powers of disposal, it seemed, were questioned that day.

And so, while we are left on shore with the memory of a deflated and stinking carcass and of bullhorns that blared and scattered us like flies, somewhere out beyond the rolled waters and the shining winter sun, the whale sings its own death in matchless, sirenian strains.

After the Storm

When, along with hundreds of others, I arrived at a barricaded Coast Guard Beach the morning after the storm, the air was full of metaphors of war. The beach, people said, looked as though it had been strafed and bombed. The line of wrecked cottages reminded some of the older men of Dresden and other European cities after World War II. From one of the remaining cottages, just beyond where the parking lot had been, the owners were hurriedly loading boxes, blankets and furniture into a waiting Jeep. Someone said they looked like a family of refugees, or a small army unit retreating from a Pacific islet. Over the beach shack a tattered flag still flew bravely. The general consensus was that the scene was one of total destruction.

The images struck me as exaggerated and inexact, though they certainly expressed the sense of awesome power conveyed by the effects of monumental tides and massive surf. But why, I thought, this emphasis on destruction? Great storms, after all, are nothing new on this beach. In 1928 Henry Beston, describing his own stay on this beach in his classic book, *The Outermost House*, wrote of 'the great northeast storm of February 19th and 20th' which, like this one, produced record tides and severe cuts in the dune walls of the barrier beach, islanding the Fo'castle, as Beston called his beach shack.

This storm, it is true, had extraordinary credentials. We were viewing the effects of what was termed 'The Storm of the

Century' and 'The Great Blizzard of '78' by the media. Two days before, on the sixth of February, an unprecedented winter storm, a hurricane in all but tropical origin, had struck southern New England, dumping thirty inches of snow on eastern Massachusetts, forty inches on Rhode Island, stranding twelve hundred commuters on Route 128 outside Boston, whose abandoned cars remained buried for several days. Car travel was banned in half the state for nearly a week, leaving many visitors marooned in expensive motels. There were several storm-related deaths, and over thirty million dollars in damage to shorefront structures in the South Shore communities of Hull and Scituate.

On the Cape fourteen-and-a-half-foot tides were measured in Provincetown Harbor during the height of the storm on Monday, and ninety-two-mile-per-hour winds were recorded at the weather station in Chatham. But except for the ever-precarious beach cottages and some heavy flooding in Provincetown Harbor, we escaped relatively unscathed, compared to the wholesale inundation, loss of life, paralyzing snowfall and severe damage inflicted on communities elsewhere on the coast.

Only on these outer barrier beaches, open to the full force of the storm surges, had the destruction been so complete. On Monday the storm had broken through the upper end of the beach, smashing apart the large National Seashore parking lot located there. The tide caught a Volkswagen lingering in the lot, swamped its engine and floated it (minus its owner) out into the marsh where it sank. The enormous waves heavily battered and undermined the public bathhouse, but the structure survived the first onslaught. The following day the massive surf rammed it again and again, while a crowd on the hill cheered with each crashing wave. (The building was finally torched by park rangers, afraid it might float off and become a navigational hazard.) The mile and a half of barrier dunes, having been weakened and set up earlier in the year by a series of powerful autumn storms, was virtually flattened. Storm surges cut sheer twenty-foot-high gouges in the dunes, and from Fort Hill across the marsh the long spit looked like a series of small mounded islands. Five of the eight remaining beach cottages were carried off. Some were totally destroyed, some had floated out and were sitting now like houseboats in the marsh, one had been carried all the way across to the town landing on the mainland side a mile to the west. One of those destroyed was the Outermost House.

I first heard about it Tuesday morning when a friend called up and asked, 'Did you hear the Outermost House perished?' All at once the storm turned serious, creating a loss that mattered. His choice of words was curiously appropriate. Its passing somehow deserved a term usually reserved for souls, thoughts and principles of human liberty.

Now I stood with the crowd, looking down the changed beach, thinking of that house, the remains of which had been scattered and swept out to sea through Nauset Inlet. Henry Beston would have understood and assented. Twenty years after his stay there 'the little house, to whom the ocean has been kind,' had already been moved back once from the beach. He had no expectations for its immortality. The house had been but the shell for the book. He knew where it was he lived.

At the end of *The Outermost House*, Beston makes his famous statement, 'Creation is here and now.' Its converse, of course, is that destruction is also here and now, and this moment it seemed to be the stronger truth. But they are really two sides of the same coin, or rather, a single indistinguishable process that human beings have divided into 'creative' and 'destructive' forces to express its effects on their own interests.

It seemed to me that the beach, looked at dispassionately, might have suggested either. The major victims of the storm appeared to be the offshore beds of sea clams, tens of thousands of which had been dragged off the ocean bottom and now lay smashed and strewn along most of the spit. As far as the gulls now picking among them were concerned, the storm meant a bounty past reckoning.

Aside from the clams, however, and a half-dozen lobster pots visible down the strand, the beaches were remarkably clean, a thousand times healthier than the lingering air of desolation and degradation that hangs over areas of human despoliation even before final abandonment and decay set in. Wide, clean plains of sand stretched across from ocean to marsh where walls of dune had stood the day before, spilling out in thick fans and pools into the marsh itself. It reminded me of old construction sites cleared away before new building began, a kind of marine urban renewal.

Often, after storms like this, the earth remembers itself. Out on those sandy plains newly-created, on the beach beyond the fragmented remains of the parking lot, I saw the curious forms of a dozen or more galvanized wellpipes sticking up out of the sand. They looked like strange periscopic life forms, some with long black noses of plastic pipe hanging from their tops, such as might be imagined on a Martian desert. Several of these wellpipes belonged to the cottages that had been swept away in the storm, but others represented former abandoned wells of the same buildings, or of others, which had been moved back or removed completely years ago.

There was also considerable evidence that erosion of the beach is not as straightforward or linear as we sometimes like to think. In one place, at the base of an eroded dune wall, a rusty old hand pump had emerged, indicating that the beach had built up some eight to ten feet since the pump was originally set. The storm had thrown up some large logs onto the beach, but it had also exposed others that had been buried in the dune wall and now stuck out from its face like huge cannons, suggesting that here, too, the beach had been much lower in a previous epoch.

An even more curious thing happened. On the way out to the beach, I had stopped at the Fort Hill overlook and scanned the outer beach across the marsh with binoculars. At the far end of the spit I spotted the blackened ribs of a small boat. It must have been exhumed by the storm, for it had not been there a week ago when I had last walked the beach. The following morning I walked the ruined beach again and could find no sign of it. Resurrected for a day, it was apparently broken up and carried off by the next high tide.

By far the most remarkable manifestation of previous lives here was just under our noses as we crowded the barricade on the road above the former parking lot. For years the asphalt bordering this road on the ocean side has been gradually crumbling away during storms. Beneath the asphalt is the surface of an earlier parking lot, and below this several feet of beach sand. Underlying the sand is a ten-to-fifteen-foot bank of clayey glacial till, reddish in color and capped with a black sticky material stepping down in layers to the beach.

Early on the morning after the storm, in the top layer of this clay till, the clawing surf had exposed the remains of two ancient Indian fire pits, about three feet across, containing rocks, charcoal, flint chips, bits of bones and other artifacts. Normally such a find would have precipitated delight and a prolonged, careful archaeological excavation with sieves and toothbrushes. In the face of the rising tide, however, no such approach was possible, and the reaction was one of controlled panic. For an instant, the sea had opened up a deep chapter in the earth's memory and would close it forever in another. Park rangers and volunteers shoveled the pits out pell-mell, hoisted their contents on boards up to the road surface and threw chunks of pre-history into a government pickup while the diggers jumped out of the way of the crashing surf. When I arrived late in the morning, the round, excavated pits, sheared cleanly into cross-sections, were still visible, but when I returned two days later to show them to a friend even the outlines were gone.

What are we to make of these fossils and artifacts, well-pipes, pumps, logs, buried ships and Indian pits? It is true that in the long run the Cape is losing ground, or at least attenuating, century by century. But along its edges, at least, the processes are not so simple. Average rates of erosion are just that, averages. Some beaches, especially at the extremes of the Outer Cape and along the Bay shores, are actually accreting and extending. But on barrier beaches such as this one, its dunes riddled with present destruction and pieces of man's forgotten past, there is an oscillation which should make us wary of classifying them too quickly as either retreating or building, for they have done both in the past and are likely to do so again.

Finally, there were impressive examples of the sea's insistence, not only on revealing human history, but on its own geologic past. In my own town, for instance, at Paine's Creek Landing, the tide broke from the Bay through a low wall of dunes, cutting a breach twenty feet wide and five feet deep into a small tidal creek that empties out of Freeman's Pond, a brackish water body further inland. A 1916 Geological Survey map shows the creek emptying into the Bay at this exact point where the cut took place. Sometime after that date the stream had been diverted westward by means of a dug trench, through a culvert that runs beneath the beach road and into the main stream, Paine's Creek. But for several months after the storm the smaller creek once more flowed in and out through its former natural channel before the cut finally filled up again.

At Race Point in Provincetown, the sea broke through the dike that was built decades ago across the inner side of Hatches Harbor, flooding the valley behind it, on whose floor the municipal airport had since been built, submerging the runways and advancing to within a few feet of the terminal building itself. By doing so it reasserted its claim to the original extent of 'Race Run,' a long, narrow, tidal estuary that flowed there in the early part of this century.

These were two dramatic examples, but there were several other instances around the peninsula where severe erosion or a cut through the dunes reminded us that this lake or that river once had different and more natural outlets.

So man makes cosmetic changes on the shoreline, building dikes and sea walls, filling in swamps and marshes, dredging harbors and rechanneling streams. But the older, deeper currents continue to run in the daily tides, like the schools of alewives that are said to swarm and beat each spring against entrances to ancestral spawning grounds that have been blocked off by man for generations. These currents carry a deep insistent earth memory that sometimes breaks out during major storms into sudden consciousness. And when the waters finally recede we are left staring across an unfamiliar landscape to redefine our human world as best we might.

A Paine's Creek Sundown

Yesterday at sunset – a cold, clear, still dawn of evening – I went down to the landing at Paine's Creek, where the herring river empties into the wide waters of the Bay. A thin band of slush ice rocked quietly against the pleated mound it was building at the edge of the tide, laving it with thin, freezing layers of wash, like a candle dipped into wax again and again. I took off one glove and dipped my hand into the dark, flaky water. It felt very cold and deep – a foreign element.

Just beyond the ice, small groups of black ducks paddled about, and a few rested lightly on the ice itself. As the ponds inland continued to freeze, more and more of these ducks would move into the estuaries and out along the shore, until their numbers would rival those of the gulls, the eiders and the brant. Occasionally a single bird, or a pair, would come winging in, fast and low, arching wings and setting legs forward like a cartoon character coming to a stop, settling in with a small flurry beside the others.

I stood atop a little sandy knoll next to the parking lot and felt myself at some universal balance point, not just of day to night, or even of the year, but of my own life and of all the myriad accompanying changes taking place around me. To the west, the familiar sweptback headland of Crowe's Pasture, with its bare, wind-shaped crest of trees, stood out in dark silhouette against a deep, fiery sun that was melting and spreading across the horizon like acrylic dyes. A wide band of dusky pink lay across the western sky, and the muted gray outline of the Sandwich power plant sent up a broad plume of smoke the same color as itself, which smeared out and leveled off at the top of the pink band, as though it had reached the limits of atmosphere, drifting south toward the melting sun. Calm as it was where I stood, there was a northerly wind not far above me, shearing down whatever rose to meet it.

All along the western horizon, far into East Dennis and beyond, that water stack, or that row of houses, that curving bend of trees – all lived in a transfiguring light, just as I, to one standing further east along the beach, must have looked transfigured. What would happen if we could all see each other so, caught in the glowing moment between the intense burning light and the cold blue shadows, out here on a wintry beach, raw and stark, yet filled with running currents of life, gilded moving forms of darkness?

To look into a sunset and then away is to look at two different worlds, so utterly different are the effects. To the east the light was simple and revealing, outlining dunes, yards, porches, roofs and fences with an almost visible edge. The windows of the deserted cottages at Brewster Park caught the sunset glow and reflected it, lighting up in response, like eyes opening, or as though orange lanterns had suddenly and simultaneously been lit from inside. The pure, clean colors of New England houses – red on yellow, blue on white – glowed with a primitivistic simplicity, making them seem at once archetypal and ephemeral, so that the absence of any human figure was appropriate.

I turned to the south and saw the gulls sailing down Stony Brook Valley, coming down from the Mill Ponds as they do each evening, cleansed of dump fever. White eyebrows against a velvet zenith, they glided effortlessly or rowed with slow, easy strokes, out past the locked mouth of the creek, past the ice-swathed beach, the band of slush ice, out beyond the black ducks, dropping down gently to settle at last with the other gulls, folding their wings like eyelids for the night.

It has always been a puzzle to me that such vulgar, raucous birds as these should be the constant witnesses of such gratuitous glories as were now taking place. But for once the gulls were silent, as though they too had been compelled out of their usual, prosaic behavior. Only a few of the larger black-backs gave low, hoarse coughs, like gruff old men grumbling in their sleep, and were answered by the ducks in soft, quacking murmurs. Further out, where the dark blue water, compressed by cold and light, appeared to flake off in shards at the horizon, I could just make out the dim patterns of larger flocks – eiders, brant, scoters, mergansers, oldsquaw, scaup and others – the undreamed hosts of waterfowl encompassed by the Bay, of which we get only the most fragmentary glimpse from shore.

I stared out across the running waters, that dark beckoning plain full of pungent and sharp smells, wandering cries, and the resurgent, far-off growl of the surf – voices, entities, elements mixing in honest solitude. Suddenly an onshore wind broke, riffling and breaking the surface of the water into a billion bits. A handful of snow buntings burst out of a clump of marsh grass like a spray of wind-blown seed and raced toward land. The air shimmered and sent a shiver through me. I was suddenly in the presence of a loud, roaring silence, rushing over me like a mountain torrent, so manifest, clear and omnipresent that I felt deaf and dumb in its grip.

Yet even as I reached out toward the edge of beauty, I found myself drawing back, unwilling to let go entirely. What is it that, even in the midst of such splendor, makes us draw back, and ultimately prefer the most banal human chatter to these wild cries, or the most tacky of human edifices to this unrelieved sweep of motion and light?

Absence of choice, I thought, is what sets this off from man. We are born fixated on choice, on the potential for shaping our environment, our lives, the future. We live in a world of discriminating, ranking, weighing, preferring, deciding, where the greatest number of options is the highest good. Individual freedom, we call it, and we will die for it.

Beauty here, however vast and compelling, is mindless. Life here, for all its marvelous adaptability and ongoing change, is caught in a matrix of forces over which it did not have, and would never have, any control. Whenever I extend myself far enough into nature, I always reach this point, where I sense 'the hollow mind of the Universe,' and my humanity catches up with me. It is this ultimate barrenness, even more than the biting sea wind, that finally chills me back into my own world.

The sun lost all form now and sank below the horizon, dragging its sea of color down after it. To the east, the eyes of the houses blinked out, going dark and hollow again. A cowl of velvet came over the white western sky, and the evening star burned steadily and brilliantly like a beacon over the departed sun. Near it, jet trails, reflecting the vanished light, gleamed like comets.

Now, on this dark beach, the lighted necklace of the Bay began to appear, diminished in winter but clearer. Far off to the northwest was a dull, indistinct glow that was Plymouth. The smoke and outline of the electric plant in Sandwich was gone now, but hard glints of light pulsed from its erect tower. Nearer, in Dennis, a green, blinking light marked the entrance to Sesuit Harbor, while a red one shone to the east for Rock Harbor in Orleans. The lights from the shore houses in Eastham, a dense strand of diamonds in summer, now strung themselves out sparsely and separately. The triple beat of Nauset Light over the Eastham plains was completely invisible, but far to the northeast the great indirect sweep of Highland Light saluted the night at twenty-second intervals. Finally, almost due north from where I stood, I could make out the inch-high pencil-thin shaft of light of the Pilgrim Monument, and the steady white light at the very tip of Long Point.

Each season has its own poetry here, given expanse enough and an unprejudiced eye. We stretch with it and draw back, but returning find our own world subtly changed and enriched. As the ducks were rocked on the slush ice, I felt rocked in those answering rhythms of the day's turning, a cradle not so much comforting as generative, suggesting an unplumbed meaning for which words like *purpose*, *order*, *design*, *end*, are not only inadequate and unsatisfactory but finally irrelevant. The landscape and seascape offer an ever-expanding range of possibilities becoming real. It may be mindless, in our analytic sense of the word, but such ordered fecundity and progressive variety seem to outstrip our very attempts to describe its limitations.

Vintage Woodland

The other afternoon I cut across the woods in front of our house to a garage on the other side where our car was being repaired. It is a piece of typical Cape woodland, mixed pitch pine and oak with a few scraggly cherry trees, still privately owned and as yet neither disturbed nor preserved by anybody, except for some evidence of bottle-digging here and there.

The land slopes and rises gently but massively. Strewn across it are great moldering boulders called glacial erratics, some twenty feet long or more, split by thousands of winters of rain and frost, covered with lichen and matted brown pine needles, decaying slowly in the winter sun. In the clefts of the rocks new saplings have occasionally taken root, widening the breaches, hastening the process of breakdown from stone into soil, soil into mold, mold into new life. What looks to the casual observer like ancient immobility is in fact a continuous process of transformation from rock into vegetable life.

But on such a day as this, a nothing-time between winter and spring, the trees themselves seemed more like stones. The 'monarchs' of these Cape woods are only thirty-five to forty feet high and barely a foot in diameter. They are all second growth, of course, and probably only fifty to sixty years old. Yet somehow in its winter barrenness, strewn with the bare wires of poison ivy, Virginia creeper and catbriar, the forest seemed much older, and infinitely remote.

In the bright cold sunshine I reached out and grasped the tight, gray, cracked trunk of a young oak with my bare hand. It was hard and unyielding, a column of vegetable reserve. I thought of its life flow, dormant now, of the continuous flow of bud, flower, seed, leaf, leaf scar. Whatever affection men may have for trees, they can never touch their hearts or feel their warmth. More coldblooded than the coldest fish, the oak stood aloof, apart from the hot, impatient demands of animal life, communicating subtly with the earth, air and rocks through the tiny orifices of root hair and stomate, the invisible pace of efflorescence, photosynthesis, denudement and dormancy. Even the skunk cabbage that burns its way up through the March snow burns with a cold and refined fire.

There are no extensive stone walls in these woods, indicating that the soil was too poor or rocky for much farming or pasturage. I suspect it was used primarily as a woodlot, until through repeated cuttings the wood quality grew so poor as to be abandoned even for this use. Here and there is evidence of old cart paths along which the wood was hauled out. And beside these are occasional small dump piles – pots, clay jugs, bits of broken plates and bottles, a rusty coal scuttle, mute indications of our ancestors' casual disposal methods. Haul in the trash, haul out the wood. Given enough time, the trash, like the boulders, would break down. With a slow enough pace, it probably qualified as a primitive recycling method – albeit an unconscious one.

I do not know how large these woods are nor who owns them. There are no deer left in them and no grouse. There is much wintergreen. They are hardly 'unique' in any way that would qualify them for special preservation, except perhaps in being so large and so close to the center of town. But it is still vintage Cape woodland, impossible to improve, beyond improvement, unique only in its dwindling representativeness of a native landscape almost unrecognized because so characteristic, speaking mutely to us, asking only, like us, to fulfill itself.

Going to Seed

There is something to be said for letting a garden go to seed. In fact, I have never quite understood such figures of speech as 'gone to seed' and 'looking seedy.' Metaphorically, they are used to imply stagnation and decay, but in nature seediness is a condition of ripeness and fruition. Where, after all, would we be if nothing went to seed?

On this late September afternoon my garden whirls and bursts with seed. All through the summer the pole bean vines rose and swung in light breezes like a green harp on the nylon webbing strung over their wooden frames. I picked and picked the pods, ripe notes off a staff, until, as Frost with his apple-picking, 'I was overtired / Of the great harvest I myself desired.' Now the long, wrinkled, paper-pale, knobby pods yield hundreds of smooth, shiny, dimpled, coffee-brown beans, more than enough for next year's planting. If I were more skilled in letting things alone, I would probably not even have to plant next spring.

The broccoli, too, has gone to seed, or at least to blossom. The secondary shoots, left uncut, have sent up spindly, curved nosegays of small, lovely, four-petaled yellow flowers visited now by black-and-yellow bumblebees with bright orange pollen sacs strapped like saddlebags to their rear legs. Examining the flowers I find that they are arranged around each curving stalk in a climbing rotation, one every 144 degrees, so that the pattern

117

is repeated every fifth blossom, or two rotations around the stem – an unexpected detail of perfection and order I should never have noticed if I had cut them as edible bud-clusters. How many other plants do we eat before they blossom?

The garden has managed to reach this unaccustomed state of seedfulness because for the last month I have not found much time for it. Had I done so it might by now have been composted, limed, rototilled and planted with winter rye in the prescribed manner, and I would never have known its rich autumn face.

Instead, lying in neglect, it has taken on a character of its own, separate from me, shaped upon the framework I gave it in the spring, but infused and animated now by another force. To a certain extent we raise a garden as we might a child, putting in the seed, nourishing it and gathering nourishment from it, pruning and weeding its growth, protecting it, loving it, worrying over it. But at some point we must let it go, and now I take a bittersweet pleasure in seeing some of my lineaments in it as it takes its own way.

There are more than beans and broccoli going to seed here. In one unmulched corner of the garden some tall, spike-leaved field thistles have invaded the perimeter. Their slender, five-foot stalks bear candelabras of white, hairy seed-tufts, milkweed-like seeds that drift across the garden like a dry snowfall, and rise up through the pitch pine branches toward white clouds and blue sky with that breath of adventure of all seasonal migrants in them.

Goldfinches visit the garden daily for these seeds, mostly the dull, yellow-green females, perhaps still feeding their late broods. They alight on the main stalks, then walk out on the side stems, curving and bending them down like boys on birches until they reach the seed-tufts. There they work at them industriously if inefficiently, shaking them loose in scattered, fugitive bursts, sending ten aloft for every one they take, dispersing the seeds even as they harvest them. Once I saw a female, finishing up a tuft, take off after the last escaping seed-ball. After a few yards' chase she snatched it on the wing like a nighthawk taking a moth.

Finches feeding on garden thistles are, I suppose, a common enough sight this time of year, but it underscored the matrix of functions that each organism, plant and animal, performs in nature. Who can say what the *main* function of any form of life is, what it is good for, or meant for, beyond perpetuating itself? We should not blame ourselves for using the earth's resources. That is not only human nature, but the nature of all things. We have no monopoly on exploitation; all life is opportunist. We ourselves, our bodies, our homes, our crops, waste and pollution are all exploited by innumerable other organisms. The error is in assuming that *our* use of any one life-form is (in the language of property-tax laws) 'the highest and best use,' and justifies the usurpation of all others. In the face of nature's own manifest multiple-use policy, such an attitude is not only dangerous but constitutes a self-defeating presumptuousness. Only through expensive, inefficient systems and carefully blindered outlooks can we manage to believe that anything grows in an exclusively human shape. Nature puts democracy to the acid test, which is perhaps one reason why Americans have for so long remained insensitive to its basic principles.

Too often, in such fevers of exclusiveness, even a garden can become a source of, rather than a refuge from, haste and anxiety. In the heat of summer I sometimes find myself rushing overheatedly from row to row, looking for signs of invasion from the surrounding woods and fields that suddenly take on the aspect of a storehouse of infinite evils.

But now in September the garden has cooled, and with it my possessiveness. The sun warms my back instead of beating on my head. No longer blindingly bright, it throws things before me into sharp relief and deepening color. The harvest has dwindled, and I have grown apart from the intense midsummer relationship that brought it on. Except for a small row of fall lettuce put in in late August, I have no vested interests now and can take what falls as manna rather than hard-earned bread.

There is a pleasure, a late-season wine, in returning here after an absence more as an observer and discoverer than a would-be master. The great August flood of foliage has subsided, and I walk through the rows finding unexpected delights and surprises: here an overlooked onion, there a delicate flowering weed, and even a volunteer cantaloupe that sprouted from a compost seed, now reaching rough-skinned fruition in the potato patch. The pairs of white cabbage butterflies still continue their pirouetting duets among the broccoli, but I am no longer compelled to join their dance, pinching their voracious green larvae off the growing plants each day. I can again take simple aesthetic pleasure in watching them, a pleasure deepened by a once and future attachment I have acquired with them.

I grow old, I grow old, the garden says. It is nearly October. The bean leaves grow paler, now lime, now yellow, now leprous, dissolving before my eyes. The pods curl and do not grow, turn limp and blacken. The potato vines wither and the tubers huddle underground in their rough weatherproof jackets, waiting to be dug. The last tomatoes ripen and split on the vine; it takes days for them to turn fully now, and a few of the green ones are beginning to fall off.

The garden air is full of the sound of crickets, the year's clock made audible, ticking off the days. I have learned that it is the black field crickets that have eaten my tomatoes in late summer, but there is still such a red flood ripening on the window sills that I do not begrudge them what they take now.

I listen to their high tripping trills, short zigzag chirps, and the searing metallic drone of the conehead grasshoppers. They provide a rhythm and a beat for the garden, their song growing slower yet somehow more urgent as the sun slants further southward through the late September skies. They themselves have no hope of surviving the season, yet they raise their communal voices in a contradictory shout, as though to warn others: 'We are running down, running down!' Spawned in summer, they are a fall sound, like the dry seed husks scraping together, the empty shells, the expended world of autumn sinking to order – dry, like death.

Yet mixed with the dry cricket song is the rich smell of marigolds which form a glow of colors around the perimeter of the garden – burnt sienna, deep orange, butter gold. The marigolds were planted late this year, but they seem more fitting as autumn flowers, when all things, even sunsets, eschew pastels. The garden is like a fire going out, dying from its center, but burning clear to the last.

It is two o'clock. The great oak to the west begins to cast its shadow across the garden as it did in March when I planted the first snow peas. Now it falls across me like a cool shroud. The warmth has gone out of the air, retreating back across space to the sun itself. Afternoons are starting to disappear once again. It is time to go in.

Beach Plum Weather

I woke up this morning thinking about beach plums. For the previous week or so the few bushes that grow along the edge of the dirt road that runs in front of our house have been ripening their stunted fruit one by one. Shaded by overhanging oaks and coated by the dust of passing traffic, they do not receive enough sun or sand (or, perhaps, salt) to bring forth a significant crop. At most, on my way out to get the mail, I pick one or two to test their ripeness and whet my appetite for a harvest elsewhere. They serve as a kind of roadside clock, a reminder that beach plums are here again, rather than the thing itself.

But it was not these berries that made me think of beach plums this morning; it was the morning itself, a whole conflux of elements coming in my bedroom window: the high, steady, strident call of a day cricket, the deep, distant blue sky above the brown-edged oak leaves, a cool cleanness in my nostrils as the air flowed in like water, the unexpected comfort and warmth of a blanket pulled up over my limbs, a sudden quiet and sense of ripe yellowness in the year – all through a three-foot-square window.

Yet all this did not say 'beach plum' in my mind so much as it triggered another set of sense memories of past pickings: of the firm, particolored fruit hanging, glowing among the dark leaves; the feel of plucking and the sound of plopping them one by one into yellow-plastic peanut butter buckets; the satisfying sight and rumble of pouring them out into the sink, like a mound of pastel glass marbles, for washing; and later, the pervasive, rich smell of cooling jelly.

Then, and only then, through the inarticulate matrix of early morning signs and the wordless rush of memories they generated, did I know, fully and awake for the first time, that the many-colored ring of beach plums had come round again, and that I must make time once more to search them out.

I suppose it was my semiconsciousness, my half-wakefulness at dawn that allowed me to be so susceptible and receptive to such an indirect but forceful process of recognizing a particular time of the year, so much more compelling than if I had merely 'remembered' it was beach plum time. But I do not think it would have happened even a few years ago, though I have been trying to live by outdoor rather than indoor clocks and calendars for some time.

I think I may, however, be attaining at last, in some small degree, a certain extension of my senses by having lived here through dozens of seasons. I do not necessarily mean by that any actual greater capacity for seeing colors or hearing sounds or smelling odors – the kind of dramatically increased perception that people forced to live for extended periods in the wilderness reportedly undergo. I am still too 'enclosed' by the comforts of civilization for that kind of forced extension.

Still less do I mean anything mystical, that sudden 'extension of self' with all surrounding natural processes that one can sometimes get floating weightlessly down a tidal creek or when suddenly overwhelmed by the rushing buoyancy of a spring day.

What I mean is something more common and constant that does not go beyond the love of things themselves, but which in the long run is more sustaining than either a practical survival knowledge or epiphanic communions with nature. It comes from a simple, growing familiarity with the elements and processes of one's natural neighborhood, so that through a conscious informed following of and attentiveness to nature, her individual signs – a bird's first song in spring, the change of the sea's color – cease to be merely detached things, pleasing perhaps but decorative merely, and are transformed into real *signs*, phonemes of a larger language which, if we cannot yet understand it fully, still catches our ear with a sense of rhythm and syntax.

More and more, as the seasons come round again, I find I am held by a myriad of small, gentle ties – the brightening of killifish in the marsh ditches, the arrival of the snow buntings, the first blood-red tupelo leaves outside my study window – that tug at me with a growing associative power that is nothing mystical, nothing beyond the love of the things themselves, but which begin to move me in the deeper rhythms of which they are a part. I begin at last to know, from practice, attachment, repetition and use, what Henry Beston meant in his shack on the Outer Beach, when he invoked 'the tremendous ritual of the year.'

Good Ghosts

In the southwestern part of our town is a large area, several hundred acres in extent, that is known locally as simply 'the woods.' These woods 'recommend themselves,' in Thoreau's apt phrase, because no one else does. They remain officially undiscovered and vulnerable, one of the last large undeveloped and unpreserved tracts of woodland left on the Cape, and as such a refuge of genuine neglect amid staged rurality, planned open space and carefully managed preserves.

Of course these woods constitute no real 'wilderness,' even in the loosest sense of the word, though even with a map it is easy to get lost in the maze of roads that cross and recross in weblike fashion throughout its extent. The roads themselves, all dirt, suggest heavy human traffic in the past and from what I have been able to glean, it has been one of the more used sections of our town. Though apparently there were never many dwellings built this far into the interior, the entire area was once a large, enclosed sheep pasture, the only remnants of which are the old names 'Eastgate' and 'Westgate' which still cling to a couple of the roads.

The terrain is typically hilly moraine, pockmarked with numerous and frequently extensive bogs and swamps which even twenty years ago had been largely abandoned, and which now have sizable pines and swamp maples growing up among the fruitless cranberry vines. Yet one can still find, partially hidden beneath catbriar thickets, decades of leaves and the camouflaging weathering of time, a network of floodgates and dikes, concrete culverts running under the roads, and several abandoned cranberry shacks, some of which were later turned into summer cottages and in their turn abandoned, too.

All this indicates that these forgotten bogs were once intensively cultivated, that large investments of time, money and human enterprise were made here. Places in the woods where four or five sandy roads now seem to meet aimlessly were once busy intersections for wagons hauling in picking equipment, mountains of boxes and families of Cape Verdean pickers from North Harwich (many of whose descendants own large parcels of the bogs today) who made these cutover woods ring with song and enterprise, where only the jay calls and the split-pear tracks of stunted deer are found today.

The only human inhabitants now are seasonal summer residents of a dozen or so 'camps' built along the shores of the string of herring ponds that border these woods. These modest houses are for the most part fairly old, some neglected, but all unpretentious and set well back from the shore so as to be nearly imperceptible from the water. As such they present a contrast to the series of recently built homes on the opposite sides of the ponds, many of which are practically cantilevered over the bluffs, their faces hanging out all year round to every passing canoe and frog.

One mild Sunday in early October our family spent the afternoon biking along the deserted roads. At one point we found a system of linked footpaths marked with weathered, wooden signs nailed to dead oaks. These bore such hand-lettered legends as 'SALLY'S ALLEE' and 'TINKER'S LANE,' named after children of a generation past whose families still summer here, though Tinker is now a banker in New York and Sally has not been down an alley in years.

The woods, I have said, are no wilderness, yet nature, being no purist, reclaims her own without prejudice. Under the short oaks the roadsides were paved with wintergreen and mayflower, and we could see the withered, brown husks of numerous ladyslippers that flourished unremarked here last June. As we pedaled along, we flushed several coveys of quail, a few grouse, and even a doe that went bounding with hard small hooves up out of a shallow kettle hole. The abandoned bogs and swamps, most of which are connected with the ponds, provide excellent breeding grounds for the thousands of herring that migrate up from the Bay each spring, as well as suitable habitats for night herons and green herons that ring the ponds in summer.

We stopped to watch the waterfowl at a narrow, wet neck of land that runs between two of the ponds. A flock of coots paddled away at our approach and several handsome little buffle-heads, or 'butterballs,' darted back and forth across the water. A pair of white-necked common loons, subdued in plumage now and a pale reminder of the wailing, brightly patterned birds I encountered on a Maine lake last summer, dove with little fillips and bobbed up again. On the far side of the pond a few canvasbacks fed quietly, an advance party, I hoped, of the hundreds of these ducks which have wintered here the past few years.

A less 'virgin' tract of woods it would be hard to find, yet it contains, more than most places, the essence of what I demand from nature. Much more than pristine wildernesses and austere mountain peaks, I crave the feeling of men *having been* in a place, of having experimented repeatedly and earnestly with it in a biodegradable way, and of having had the grace and good sense to abandon it when it was no go, leaving no permanent scars, only good ghosts and a fine wildlife habitat. These woods have that sense of human depth to them as few places I know. Even the trees themselves, scraggly rather than primeval, show signs of recent ravagement by gypsy moths, a human import.

It is this kind of connection with the land that I think we most want. We desire, at bottom, neither a subjugation of nature nor a self-segregation born of a fear of our own destructiveness, but rather that intermingling of man and his environment, a land held truly in common, that produces the truest, richest natural history. Not only our numbers, but our notions of ownership and use, seem to have grown to the point where we can no longer afford such 'places of enlightened neglect,' as a friend of mine calls them. We must either appropriate them forever into some irrevocable human shape, or else quarantine them off for some sort of 'passive recreational use.'

I myself have put a good deal of time into trying to acquire or preserve just such areas for official conservation use. As a conservationist, I know that either we must manage them or they will be managed for us in not too many years. Yet I still cannot help but feel that there is a certain sterility, or stasis, that is shared by restored windmills and national parks, where all conceivable activities have been programmed, regulated or prohibited – in a word, circumscribed. I suppose it is that any place from which we have deliberately removed our full engagement is, in a sense, no longer natural.

In such a polarized world, with all its lines drawn, a place like this, still so anonymously and indefinitely designated as 'the woods,' remains valuably alive, open-ended and open to all universal forces, natural and human. It is one of those diminishing number of places on earth whose fate has not yet been pigeonholed one way or the other. Because it remains alive in this way, it is almost tremblingly vulnerable. Yet because of its vulnerability it retains, for a little while at least, the enriching possibility of something further (though probably something final) happening here of which we are a living part.

Thinning the Woods

.

Chain saws are everywhere now, and there is no getting away from them. Over the past few years the whine and growl of their unfettered engines have become a characteristic sound in our November woods, muffling or shutting out some of the other seasonal sounds, chipmunk calls or the bugling of geese breaking away overhead.

I am as guilty as anyone of adding to this raw fall combustion when I go out to cut next year's firewood. Once the leaves are off the trees, I head out with my chain saw, gas can, chain oil, socket wrench, safety goggles and ear plugs in hand, ready to confront nature in a manner that often seems as alien and removed as flying a jet plane. For twenty minutes at a time the air is filled with a geared thunder that obliterates all perception, and at the same time spawns a sense of power that is both exhilarating and frightening.

It is, in fact, an incomprehensible feeling, a madness, really, like driving a car or falling in love. You are at once in possession of and possessed by a mighty force that you fool yourself into believing you control. You read the manuals, follow the directions, and in minutes living things which have stood firm and tall against hurricanes, blizzards and gypsy moths for fifty years or more lie about you in heaps like giant crooked veins, and the sky overhead is suddenly, inexplicably open. If I can do *this*, you think, in less than half an hour, think what ten thousand of these saws, working eight hours a day across much of Maine and the Pacific Northwest, can wreak!

Still, it pays to be practical about madnesses, to drive with consideration and to reserve honeymoon suites. I do most of my cutting in my neighbor's woods, a large tract of typical Cape scrubby oak, a portion of which he kindly allows me to clear each year. The first year I harvested these trees I asked myself, what was the best way to cut them, both to maximize their yield and improve their quality? Before starting, therefore, I called the state forester in Carver, who drove down the following week and gave me advice on which trees to cut, which to leave, what density they should be thinned to, etc., assuring me that with proper management these woods could yield several cords of oak logs annually on a sustained yield basis.

So I began to thin the woods, and soon found myself a victim of conflicting claims. For these were not only woods from which I sought to harvest firewood, but also woods I frequently enjoyed for their own sake. The problem was, how to take out what I wanted, and yet leave what I wanted? On the most super-ficial level, some of the most obvious candidates for cutting were the most visually interesting trees. These were the so-called 'wolf trees' which, in the forester's view, took up too much of the forest canopy for the amount of wood they produced. Wolf trees are those with low, wide-spreading crowns, often with multiple trunks and grotesquely warped branches, as opposed to the straight, tall, single-boled, high-branching trees preferred by foresters and, presumably, by me, the woodgatherer.

Such trees, I was told, were 'bleeding' the forest, useless not only for lumber but inefficient producers of firewood as well. On the other hand, they possessed to my eyes a valuable character, not only one of natural sculpture, but a concrete expression of survival in the face of past battles – fierce competition, repeated cutting, the loss of leaders from browsing, chronic fires, insect infestations, wind damage – all of which, like stoic soldiers, they did not speak, but mutely bore the scars and mutilations of their endurance. Yet in terms of firewood, which I needed, these were bad trees.

'Take out the snags,' the forester said, 'and watch out for signs of damage, broken or dead limbs. Chances are the rot has spread down through the trunks.' So the dead, the sick and the dying should be weeded out, to make more room for the healthy. It was not anthropomorphic sentimentality that made me hesitate here, but some knowledge of what role these 'damaged' trees play in the broader life of the forest: providing abundant insect food for woodpeckers, nuthatches, warblers and other birds; nesting cavities for chickadees, titmice, screech owls, wood ducks, squirrels and other animals.

One never knows what one is getting into, or getting rid of, with such trees. Once, cutting through a foot-thick oak trunk that proved to be hollow, I sawed right through an occupied mouse nest, severing one of the inhabitants not-so-neatly in two. My cutting partner that day quipped something about 'If ever there was a mouse whose time had come . . . ,' but we were both somewhat shaken by the experience. Even standing dead stumps play unsuspected roles in the forest community. I have found as many as a dozen salamanders hibernating around the base of one old hulk whose bark I peeled off like so much wrapping paper.

There is also something about thoroughly 'managed' forests that suggests, if not sterility, at least a certain lack of possibility. I distrust them, and those who assure us we can have wilderness and lumber together forever, in the same way that I distrust 'reclaimed' trout ponds. For all the deer in one, or trout in the other, something, some unpredictableness, some variety of experience has been excised in the process of management. The point is, do we want something out of our forests and ponds besides a 'maximum sustained yield' of fuel and fish? Through years of benevolent neglect by their owner, these woods have produced something else – call it a certain completeness, for lack of a more precise term – that I was reluctant to remove. There were parallels here with the human community, of course, but the whine of my chain saw would not let me pursue them too far.

There were broader considerations as well, matters of species preference, for instance. The woods I was thinning are largely oak, but also contain some pitch pine, white pine, red maple and small stands of beech, as well as scattered spruce trees which, although planted years ago by my neighbor, are still only a few feet high after several decades. Should I thin out the maples and the pines, both of which have lower fuel values than the oak, thereby growing more BTUs per acre? But the pines support red squirrels and pine siskins, invite hermit thrushes and crossbills, and give the deer a place to bed down in blizzards. The maples give a certain glow to the autumn woods that the duller oaks lack, and also yield me modest amounts of maple syrup in the spring. Besides, a too homogeneous forest, such as this oak monoculture, is one of the primary reasons that it has been so susceptible to insect attacks such as those of the gypsy moth over the years. These other species represent a natural attempt at diversity, nature's proven strategy against ecological disaster. Shouldn't I keep them, then? Perhaps even let some sun into the alien spruce trees, which might otherwise sit forever beneath the native oaks, and so encourage artificial variety?

I was suddenly confronted by a wilderness of choices more perplexing than the most pathless woods. By giving me leave to cut selectively some of his woods as I saw fit, the owner had to some degree given me stewardship over its character. What I soon realized was that, in thinning these woods, I might very well be thinning myself.

What, after all, was a 'good' tree or a 'bad' one? In comparison to what? It depends on what we want from them. Some trees, like the giant Sequoias, are considered best for feeling small next to. Others, like the seas of Douglas firs in Oregon, are generally valued most highly as potential plywood sheets for sheathing our homes. Spruce in Maine are potentially good newspapers. The scrub oak on our ocean bluffs are probably best left as natural erosion controls, as are the mangrove swamps in Florida. About some, like the California redwoods, we may not yet have made up our minds.

But what about these woods right here? How should I handle them, see them? Should I designate certain areas as 'managed' and others as 'wild'? Does that make sense when I am talking half acres instead of square miles? Should I liberate this young white pine from the surrounding oaks because it makes such a handsome shape against the sky, or encourage the beeches for their smooth limbs and their sweet nut crops that the local grouse forage on? This broken-down oak may be a 'bad' tree to leave standing, but an excellent one to climb. Dear neighbor, what am I supposed to do with all this?

The problem, you see, is one of proximity. If this were

just any woods, I might be able to put on my blinders and see every tree as potential stove logs, and so have no problem. Better yet, if I could afford to have my wood trucked in from some distant wood lot in New Hampshire, I would have to consider these questions even less. Only a few years ago – centuries, it seems now – I could simply have my oil shipped in from some anonymous Middle Eastern country or the Mexican gulf and not have to think about such things at all.

But I can't. These woods are where I live, and I want so many different things from them – including a certain practical necessity. What is a 'good' tree, therefore, depends. It not only depends, it changes, as I do. It is the same with our planet as a whole, and perhaps the best thing to come out of the whole energy crisis will be that we will be forced, in one way or another, back to our sources, away from the isolation and compartmentalization of function that an arrogant, man-dominated view of life has fostered, back to the realization that we all want essentially the same things from the same place, that the earth, like these woods, is where we live.

How did I finally thin the woods? In part I compromised, and in part I was compromised by the woods themselves. I left some of the wolf trees, some damaged and some dead ones, and took others. I liberated some of the white pines and left others to battle for themselves. I encouraged the beeches but decided that the spruces would have to wait for a natural opening. After all, the gods have always been capricious.

As for which areas to thin and which to leave, the lay of the land itself pretty much decided that. Most of the woods grow on fairly steep morainal hillsides. On one side of the road it is fairly easy to cut trees a good distance up the slope and drag or roll them down to my vehicle. On the downslope side, which descends into a deep wooded hollow, I have found it is not usually worth going much more than twenty or thirty feet off the road. Curiously enough, I have found evidence that others before me have reached the same conclusion, for the largest trees on the property tend to be growing on the lower levels of the hollow, though that may have something to do with less wind and more moisture as well. At any rate, since I do not work with mechanized tree harvesters and helicopters, but am still, like previous woodgatherers here, on a one-to-one, albeit more noisy basis with each tree I cut, those in the hollow will remain untouched, an 'unmanaged' area where the wood ducks and screech owls may still find trunk cavities in which to raise their young and the woodpecker may tattoo his winter song on the dead but resonant limbs.

Return to the Dunes

I climb the thickly vegetated ravine that lies between two rounded, sandy flanks on the eastern slope of Mt. Ararat, up from the National Seashore's parking lot that once served as a siding for the railroad into Provincetown. Winter is the best time for exploring the dunes – the sands are firmer, the walking easier. It has been cold and still for the past several days, and it is like walking over slightly sanded concrete, leaving no footprints. Relatively few people seek out the dunes in winter, and one can walk an entire day without seeing another soul.

Ararat is a good vantage point from which to begin. From the summit one has a commanding view to the west of a series of roughly parallel dune ridges, stretching away in a spray of gradually diverging lines toward Race Point and Hatches Harbor. Geologists believe that these ridges, which they call 'relict spits,' represent former shorelines of the Provincetown Hook, which has been gradually building farther and farther out into the Atlantic over the past five thousand years or so. To the east, north of Pilgrim Lake, are the so-called 'parabolic dunes,' a striking belt of dunes in the shape of strongly bent bows, all remarkably regular in shape and all oriented, one behind the other, from northwest to southeast. These were also originally formed by material thrown up from the sea, but now belong totally to the wind, wind-gathered and wind-shaped.

Some have chided the name Ararat as pretentious for a hundred-foot sand hill, which is not even very large as world dunes go, but I think the connotations are appropriate enough. The dunes themselves, as I have said before, have a powerfully Biblical aspect. Ararat is as barren as the eminence the ark is said to have stranded on, and it looks down on a landscape strangely transformed, where the bristly tips of still-living trees and the blackened skeletons of dead ones protrude from the inundating sands, giving a sense of bleakness and prostration as great as must have met Noah's eyes when he viewed the wreckage of flood-drowned forests. The prospect speaks at once of failure and new promise: from here the world can be made new or wrecked again.

Both the dunes and I have undergone many changes – I more than they – since I first visited them in comparative ignorance in the early sixties. To the southwest, across Route 6, Ararat's companion dune, Mt. Gilboa, has been truncated to provide a base for one of the town's water standpipes. Each winter the southern slope of Mt. Ararat tries to move across the highway, and each winter the state road crews scrape up the sand and pack it back up against the dune. Eventually the sands may become vegetated enough so that they will stay where men want them to, but stabilization is a slow process, even with beach grass plantings, and the dune seems in no hurry to give up its mobility.

Nowadays Geographical Survey maps usually accompany my walks. I take one out of my pocket and open it to check my bearings. Almost immediately a sharp gust of wind tears it from my gloved hands, sending it tumbling and flapping over the crest, and I am forced to limp after it down the steep slopes in awkward, undignified pursuit. I finally overtake it and stuff it back in my pocket. Admonished, I head north across valleys and ridges, toward the ocean that is a little over a half-mile away.

Here and there the clean ivory flanks of the sand are striated with long, snaking lines of dark soil, usually interrupted, but sometimes forming wide, meandering circles. These are remnants of former growth, thickets and tree stands now totally gone except for these thin bands of sandy loam they laid down when alive. Rarely are the bands more than a few inches wide, for the vegetation here does not grow on flat plains, but drapes itself over the domed dune-tops or lines the bowllike hollows. Later, only selected edges are reexposed by the shifting sands, running like contour lines along the flanks of the dunes.

The dunes are deserts in appearance only. A wide variety of plant and animal life attests to the abundance of moisture here. Stands of stunted, mature pitch pine and planted jack pine lie hidden like small green lakes in the sheltered valleys. The domesticity of life in these forest outposts, already being buried alive, is touching. Rabbits dart in secret, weaving between the close trunks. Yellow-flecked myrtle warblers flit in their branches. Piles of cone bracts lie at their bases where red squirrels have been feeding, and the trees huddle close while their fallen cones are washed together by the wind, like mounds of shells on a remote beach.

These pines tend to occupy the more protected areas, while the scrub oaks, being more windfirm and salt-tolerant, have colonized many of the dune crests, and have even given their name to one: Oak Head. Crows, black and gigantic, land in their miniature crowns. Flocks of snow buntings bank and swing with a metallic chittering over the dune tops. A marsh hawk cruises low, following the undulating contours of the valleys.

The dune hills, born of wave and shaped of wind, are made of material clawed by the ocean from the outer beach cliffs of Truro and Wellfleet to the south, then transported north by longshore currents to be added to the fist, or hook, of the Provincelands. As such they are the finely mixed and blended grist of glacial deposits – homogenized geology. Yet not completely. Even here the earth is sorted and distilled. Because of variations in wind velocity, the predominant quartz of the sand is sometimes interspersed with very thin layers of lighter material, purplish magnetite, for instance – an aping of the stratified glacial layers in which it once lay. I pick up a handful of sand and see a multitude of colors in its individual grains, grains so numberless they trivialize cosmic time, saying that the infinitude of matter is more than a match for the forces that destroy and reshape it.

The dune ridges, and their intervening valleys, suggest the crests and troughs of waves beating toward a beach. Like waves, they also move, though much more slowly. Yet where waves, once set in motion, move by an inner energy, the dunes are moved from outside, by the wind. They shift by incremental movements of their individual grains in leaping bounds, a process known as *saltation*, literally, 'a dancing.' These wind-driven grains hit and move other grains, creating a second type of movement called *surface creep*. It is all like an enormously complex game of billiards, or a sluggish nuclear chain reaction. Even now there is a low misting of sand grains around my ankles. The horizons of the dune crests are slightly blurred with their movement, as though this were all a mirage. I walk in a moving river of sand.

Such mutability is an affront and a threat to our modern need for stability in nature, a need that grows in proportion to our own increasing mobility. Our sense of motion used to come from the movement of clouds overhead, or of the tides on the beach, or of the seasons through the fields and forests. Now we outstrip the clouds, seek to arrest the effects of tide and wave, and can follow the seasons at our will, in pursuit of endless summer.

I suppose this is one reason that we tend to feel that places like this are capricious, a 'playground' for human pleasure, where nothing serious or important ever happens. We regard it only when it suits our limited purposes, which is largely why it still has so much life of its own and has retained so little of man –only a deserted hunting blind on top of one of the oak-encrusted knolls, or the thigh bone of a cow exposed at the bottom of one of the sand bowls.

The bottoms of most of these bowls, or hollows, lie at or near sea level, and during winter and spring almost all of them contain some amount of water, exposed portions of Provincetown's meager water table. Some are quite temporary, small clean-bottomed pools of fresh water, clear and sweet to the taste. Others have long reddish vines of wild cranberry trailing around their edges. The more permanent of these dune wetlands have evolved into semi-swamps, full of sedge, alder, blackberry, blueberry, and dense bayberry stands heavy with their blue winter fruit. In one of these the surprisingly large local deer herd has come to drink quite recently; I read fear and alarm in their numerous, confused tracks, and wonder how such large animals manage to disappear so completely out here.

Finally I gain the beach, where white-toothed breakers tear like buzz saws through the blue water toward land. Offshore, a weatherbeaten dragger plows homeward, toward Race Point, trailing a thousand-foot scarf of screaming gulls behind it. The sun slants over my left shoulder – it is beginning to grow colder. I think this is roughly where Harry Kemp's dune shack once stood, the little house in which I took refuge on that winter night years ago. It has long since fallen into the sea, and there are no others in the vicinity. Besides, I am too grown now, too sympathetic to trespass laws to attempt another such adventure, too full of maps to get lost, and too bound by invited responsibilities to try.

So I head back the way I came, the dune ridges now back-lighted and casting their long purple shadows across the valley floors. Over the years I have learned something of their geology, a little of their ecology, less of their behavior and almost nothing of their mineralogy, and have from time to time come upon unexpected bits of human history among their seemingly barren wastes. What I have learned has made their terrain much more dense than it was, a playground for the mind as well as the body. I can trace their contours more accurately now, but in their actual presence this knowledge slips away like the map torn out of my hands by the wind, and I do not begin to know what to make of them. They seem to be more than we can know and more than we can imagine, offering us a place in which to test our own abilities to change, to move like them in new directions, burying the old life and bringing forth the new.

Common Ground

At 5:30 PM, after a very businesslike day and expecting little more, I drove down to Nauset Beach, realizing with some surprise that I had not been there in months. In early April the dry beach grass and tasseled seed-heads still dominated the dune crests, but at the base of the plants I could see sharp, thin, green blades already several inches long starting up among the dead stems, tough little cactuslike clusters of dark-pointed spikes that made the rounded dunes before me look like the backs of giant porcupines.

There is an aggressiveness, a territoriality in this plant, a hard new thrust rather than a soft spring, as though to say, 'Whoever would disturb my growth had better be pretty hard-soled.' In its deep, gridlike roots that shove six feet or more down into the sand, in its ability to withstand a foot or more of sand burial each year, in its preference to spread by runners rather than seed, there shows an unwillingness to give up its original site, whether from above, below or to the side. The beach grass, compass grass, stands, its seed-head high and straight, its long, bent blades fingering in the sand the bold and ancient act of circumscription: Here, here am I!

Suddenly this beach hit me again in all its unimaginable simplicity of grandeur, the rolling and tilting planes of sand, so tenacious and so yielding. The sea itself, though the tide was coming in, was strangely calm and peaceful. It curled low and thoughtful against the lower beach as though, if it knew, it were giving no inkling of the human tides that would soon descend upon its shores. There were only five or six other walkers in the mile-or-so sweep of beach visible; a good human distance, I thought, that relieved each of us from the obligation of any semblance of purpose or response or expression for what we were doing there or of what we saw, and left us individually to gather, if we could, the bloom of this incipient season, here in the light of the dying sun.

As I walked north, flocks of sea ducks, heavy and low on the water, flew in long straight lines beyond the breakers, which fell softly in long, glistening, unbroken curls, like giant strands of silver kelp. In further, between the breaking swells, a bird that looked like a loon dove and rose, over and over, seeming to flip out of sight each time just as I fixed my sight on it, as though it could feel the touch of my eyes at a hundred feet. (Many waterfowl seem to be able to do this.)

I will come back tonight, I thought, to see if the plankton bloom has come ashore yet, to walk this black beach and be star-shod again with minute phosphorescent marine organisms, those invisible, innumerable necessities of the sea, the vast and fragile foundation on which our own and all other lives rest.

When the shadows of the dunes at last began to cover me, I stopped and climbed through a break in their line, heading back toward the parking lot. I walked easily now, more than satisfied, even asking silently for no more, afraid that it would be wasted or spilled carelessly. The sun slanted across the inner slopes of the dunes, shadowing swales and depressions in the sand with a pale blue-gray shading, washing the dune slope above me with a rosy luster. A single footprint in the sand gives this same striking suffusion of tints. Nothing shows nature's indifference to man's desires more than this negligent overflow of beauty. Even more than random cruelty, it is an affront to our expectations and to our sense of deserts. But it is also a symptom of the earth's abundance, her healthy and generous disposition, which leads one to look upon any disappointment or loss as insignificant, as a spot too keenly or exclusively focused on.

I followed the sand tracks leading between the spreading mats of poverty grass and beach grass, leaving lines of deepening prints behind me. My life is no more certain than it has ever been, balanced on points that are as precarious as any rabbit's or sand flea's. And yet I have been more sure this past week of its current, its gravitation toward this place, than I have been all year. Once more I felt as though I could beg to live here.

On the way back I passed the small reed-bordered pond (I call it Nauset Pond, since it seems to have no other name) that lies just in back of the dunes. Its waters are brackish, not surprisingly, since it is less than one hundred fifty feet from the high-water mark on the beach, separated from the ocean only by a line of twenty-foot dunes. If the hydrologists are to be believed, the pond floats on a bed of sea water that infuses up into the sand from below. In fact, the pond level does appear to fluctuate somewhat with the tides. Now a pair of mallards were feeding in the shallows among the dense stands of cattails that were mounted with noisy swaying flocks of blackbirds, newly arrived, their red shoulder patches flashing and growing brighter as their songs grew louder and more constant. On the far side of the pond stood a great blue heron, motionless as a spear of driftwood, but ready at any second to take off and assume its sculpted flying form.

To the west I caught a glimpse of a bird in brilliant silhouette, flapping low and hawklike above the inner dunes. Possibly a pigeon hawk, I thought – and all at once I was reminded with sudden force of another hawk I had found and chased on this beach nearly ten years before. It was a morning in late fall, at a time when I seemed cast off from my life and stranded naked on these shores. Then I had followed the bird around the pond for nearly half an hour, chasing it from perch to perch with a desperate appreciation and forced curiosity. I hung on its every tilt and veer as onto a fragile but vital conversation, seeking in every detail and nuance of its identity some communion, direction and purpose for my own presence here.

What the pigeon hawk had taught me that day, though I could not afford to admit it to myself then, was the limits of nature's capacity to supply the needs of the human heart. It may and does extend and clarify our lives, but it cannot be a substitute for them. The superior life does seem to lie in reaching out beyond ourselves, even beyond the human community toward universal recognition; but as Shaw recognized, you can't talk religion to a man with bodily hunger in his eyes. It was finally the bread of human intercourse, without which none of us survives for long, that sustained me throughout that long winter of uncertainty and eventually allowed me to prepare for a new life here.

Fulfillment seems to come only when it is not necessary. The things I saw this afternoon on the beach – the emerging beach grass, the dark tapestry of lichen and moss on ground of old ivory, the diving loon, the pond with its ducks and blackbirds, the hawk – all these, I realized, were not necessary points on which to hang my day, though in one sense they heightened, colored and enriched it beyond measure. Rather, they were releases, extensions and complements of my own current pre-occupations with truculent sewage pipes, committee meetings, newspaper deadlines, food for my son's salamander, car brakes, and a hundred other everyday concerns that were a result of my living here in earnest with others of my own kind.

Like the pigeon hawk, I, too, now implied a landscape, though it might be a too-human one, one that needs leavening and allying with that more inclusive natural one. I carried more weight around with me now than I had during my first encounter with the hawk. But these things had become my roots, sinking deep, and putting me on an equal footing, or perch, with it. So that as we passed one another, going in opposite directions across the pond, I felt a kinship with the hawk that might last the rest of my days here.